THE ESSENTIALS OF
HORSEMANSHIP

THE ESSENTIALS OF
HORSEMANSHIP

JOCELYN DRUMMOND

Howell Book House
New York

This book is not intended as a substitute for professional advice and guidance. A person should take part in the riding activities discussed in this book only under the supervision of a knowledgeable person. Furthermore, the book is not intended as a substitute for medical advice of licensed veterinarians. The information is provided for the purposes of education and to give as complete a picture as possible. The reader should consult a veterinarian in matters relating to his or her horse's health and particularly in regard to any symptoms that may require diagnosis or medical attention.

All pictures are the property of Regency House Publishing with the exception of those on pages 8 top, 12–13, 15 bottom right, 16, 17 bottom right, 23 top, 27, 35 right, 43, 44–45, 46 both, 47 top and bottom, 53 bottom two left, 54 both, 56 top, 57 bottom, 60 bottom, 83, 90, 91 top, 92, 93, 99, 100, 101, 102, 103, 104, 105, 106 top which are by courtesy of Kit Houghton Photography.

Howell Book House
A Simon & Schuster Macmillan Company
1633 Broadway
New York, NY 10019

MACMILLAN is a registered trademark of Macmillan, Inc.

Library of Congress CIP data available from the Library of Congress

ISBN 0-87605-669-9

Printed in Italy
1 0 9 8 7 6 5 4 3 2 1

Page 2
The author exercising her Danish warm-blood, Triton.

Page 3
Building a relationship with your horse is a rewarding and enjoyable experience. This horse and owner are happy and contented in each other's company. However, the horse really should be wearing a headcollar!

Above
Horses develop their own attachments in the field and in the stable yard. They have amazingly good memories and always remember an equine friend, even when re-united after many years.

Right
Horses come in many builds and sizes, from the lightweight Thoroughbred to the shire-horse. This cob suits her rider and is working well in the manège.

CONTENTS

INTRODUCTION

The Essentials of Horsemanship
*is for people who love horses and wish to care for them and ride them to
the best of their ability. Even if you do not have a horse of your own but use
the facilities of a riding school, it is essential to lay good foundations in
order to become a good rider later on. Particular attention is paid to details
which can be overlooked in the normal course of events and a variety of tips
and helpful suggestions are provided. Remember, however, that it takes
many years of tuition, patience and application to reach your ultimate goal.
This is designed to speed up the process and at the same time complement
any regular instruction you may already be receiving.*

*Horses are complex and sensitive creatures, as easily upset by inappropriate
feeding as they are by ill-fitting saddlery, both of which can make them
uncomfortable if not actually unwell. Even grooming, if performed
incorrectly, can present potential hazards to both horse and handler. Never
forget that horses are individuals, with distinct personalities and special
talents of their own. Ignorance can be the cause of inadvertant cruelty:
therefore it is important to seek advice and take appropriate action
whenever a problem occurs. These days, riders may find themselves
bombarded with 'expert' advice and persuasive advertising, much of it
contrary to traditional practice. This is an up-to-date, sensible approach
which does not, however, seek to abandon tried and tested methods.*

*Choosing the right horse takes time and all the advice you can get,
especially if you are a novice, and there is much to be considered – from
conformation, performance and temperament to the price you are willing to
pay, both in terms of time as well as hard cash. Once you have made your
purchase, stable management, choice of tack, clipping and shoeing – all
need to be carefully studied. You will notice a close relationship developing
which should prove interesting and rewarding for you both, as long as you
treat your horse with both tact and fairness right from the start. You will
notice his strengths as well as weaknesses while never losing sight of your
own. The day will finally come when all your hard work finally pays off and
you succeed in your first competition – horse and rider in perfect harmony.
Above all, be open-minded and adaptable.*

Chapter One
LOOKING AT HORSES: CONFORMATION

Horses come in all sorts of shapes and types and there are many oddly-shaped animals which are nevertheless much loved and do a creditable job of work. The fact remains, however, that an animal which is well put together, with correct conformation, is more likely to be in balance and move well, be an athletic performer and stay sound.

Specific breeds, for example Arabs or native ponies, have very strict requirements for breed 'type': this means the particular features which characterize the breed. Seeing a number of horses of different breeds together will help you recognize good and bad examples as well as teaching you to distinguish one from the other. Although the make and shape will of course vary according to the breed or type, and the job it is meant to do, all the main criteria for good conformation will still apply.

When assessing conformation, stand well back and look first at the overall picture. Is the horse in proportion or does he look like two different horses stuck together in the middle? When the horse is standing on level ground the

Above

In the show ring, the conformation of a particular type or breed of horse is of paramount importance. Other factors, such as condition, temperament and fluidity of movement are also assessed. This is a quality show hunter.

Right

Most performance horses, as we know them today, stem from the English Thoroughbred. The head is easily recognizable, combining an alert expression, small neat ears, a kind eye and an intelligent look.

Opposite below

This pony is lacking the kind of conformation considered vital for the show ring: in particular, his shoulder and pasterns are rather upright, but he is a workmanlike mount for any child. Many native breeds are very strong and sturdy and may present problems for small children who have difficulty controlling them. This pony, however, is neither too heavy nor too lightweight.

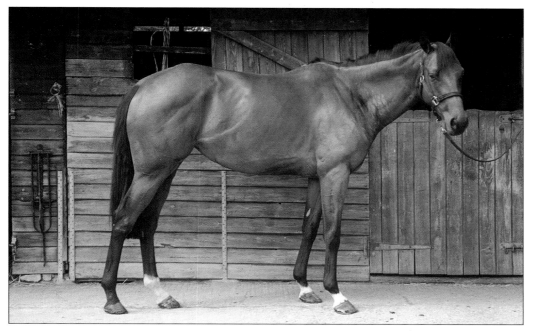

Left
This young Thoroughbred mare is rather light of bone with long cannon bones. Her lack of muscle and 'ewe neck' will be considerably improved with correct training and feeding.

Below
When assessing a horse's conformation, pay particular attention to the limbs. This horse has straight limbs, strong-looking joints, plenty of bone and well-balanced feet.

Below left
Here is an example of a horse with a fine Roman nose. This is not a conformation defect but an inherited feature, passed down through certain breeds.

withers and the point of the croup should be level. A horse that is 'croup-high' will feel 'downhill' to ride. Compare the length of the leg and the depth of the body; a shallow-bodied animal will lack strength and stamina.

The head, neck and shoulders Look for large, kind and fairly wide-set eyes in a broad forehead. Small piggy eyes with a bump between them can sometimes, though not always, indicate a tendency to bad temper. Are the nostrils wide and can you fit your fist between the jaw bones? If so, the horse will have plenty of breathing space when exerted.

The head should match the size of the body and neck. The horse uses his head as a balancing mechanism so an over-large head will over-weight his forehand. The neck should appear to grow out of the top of the shoulder, arching gently towards the poll, and attach to the head (the 'set' of the

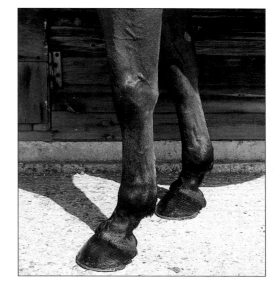

head and neck) at an angle that will allow the horse to flex comfortably. This leads to good natural 'self-carriage' which is an asset in any sphere and particularly important for dressage and showing. It is important that the angle is not too acute or the jowl too thick. Conversely, there is the neck which looks as though it is set on upside-down with an over-developed underside and obvious dip and lack of muscle in front of the withers. This is known as a 'ewe neck'. The horse will naturally carry its head too high and adopt a hollow outline, making schooling and control much more difficult. A low-set neck gives the rider a feeling of going downhill, while horses with short thick necks, especially if the under-neck muscles are over-developed, find it easy to pull against the rider's hand and difficult to carry themselves in a correctly rounded outline. A neck that is thin and weak, especially behind the poll, will allow the horse to over-bend.

The angle of the shoulder is very important. A long sloping one (45-50° to the ground is ideal) acts as a shock absorber. It will give a comfortable ride and, combined with a well-set head and neck,

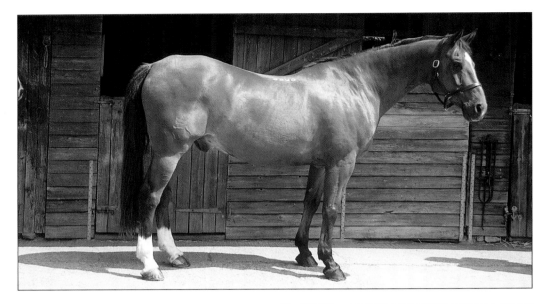

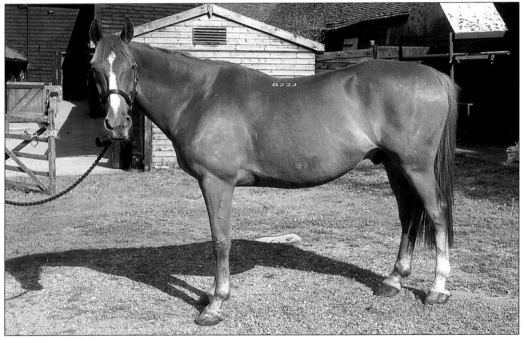

will give the feeling of 'a good length of rein'. An upright shoulder gives a jarring, short-striding ride, and combined with a low-set neck can leave the rider feeling as though there is nothing out in front of them. Well defined withers are ideal and usually go with a good shoulder. Low, fleshy, withers (often seen in ponies, cobs and Arabs) and high bony ones (common in Thoroughbreds and older horses) both make fitting saddles difficult.

The back should be strong and straight and not too long. A very short back may affect the length of stride and the horse will be more likely to over-reach or forge. A long back, though comfortable, can be weak, especially if it dips behind the saddle area (called a 'sway back'). This often develops in old horses. An upward arch in this area ('roach back') is uncomfortable and affects the freedom of movement. The width needs to be in proportion to the rest of the animal, with plenty of room for muscle development. From the side, the girth measurement should be as deep as possible with 'well sprung' ribs. A horse lacking in depth with 'slab sides' (flat rib cage) will lack space for the lungs and therefore stamina, especially if the chest is also narrow. He may also be 'herring gutted', lacking depth towards the back of the rib cage with a large gap between the last rib and the hip-bone. Horses like this are difficult to keep looking in good condition, both because of their inherent shape and because there is less room for the contents of the abdomen.

Still looking at the side view, the hindquarters should always be as long as possible from the croup to the point of the buttocks. This allows for plenty of muscle attachment and subsequent power and strength. Ideally, the quarters should be as level as possible, with the tail set quite high and carried well. A sloping hindquarter (a 'goose rump') can be a sign of a good jumper but short round, apple-shaped quarters are most undesirable. A tail clamped down or carried to one side may be a sign of discomfort or back trouble.

Now look at the horse front-on. He should look neither over-wide ('bosomy') nor as though 'both legs come out of the same hole'. Are his limbs straight? Any crookedness will throw extra

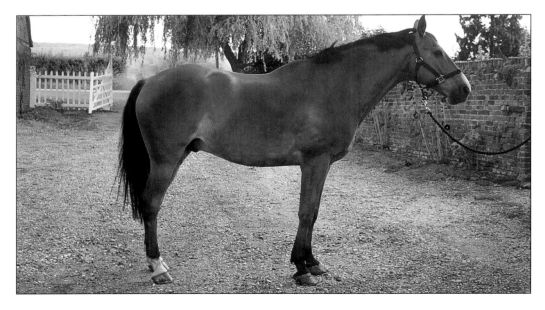

strain onto the limbs and joints. From the side, the leg should be straight with big flat-boned joints for strength and good shock absorption, with plenty of room for muscle attachment. Puffy ill-defined joints are a sign of weakness and/or wear and tear. 'Back at the knee' conformation puts strain on the back of the leg, in particular the tendons. Being 'over at the knee' rarely causes problems unless very marked and a sign of wear and tear.

Can you fit a fist between the elbow and the rib cage? If so, the fore-limb should be able to move freely. A long, well-muscled fore-arm denotes power and freedom of movement, while the distance between the knee and fetlock should be relatively short for strength. The flexor tendons, which should be clean-cut, will then also be short and less prone to strain. The pastern absorbs shock in a similar way to the shoulder and should be at the same angle (ideally 50°). A short, upright pastern will mean a short, jarring stride while a very long one will lack strength and put too much strain on the flexor tendons.

The term 'bone' means the measurement around the leg just below the knee and in fact includes the tendons, ligaments and other soft tissue. It is one way of assessing a horse's weight-carrying ability, a horse that has plenty of 'bone' being likely to carry more weight than one of the same size that is 'light of bone' or 'tied under the knee'. The hard, flat bone of Thoroughbred, Arab and other quality horses is stronger than the less dense, round bone of more common horses. Of course, the rest of the horse's build and conformation also needs to be taken into account.

From behind we are again looking for symmetry. The points of the hips should be level, with sufficient width for good muscle development. Look for broad, well-muscled second thighs with no appearance of the horse being 'split up' behind. The old adage that a horse should have 'a head like a duchess and the bottom of a cook' holds true. A plumb-line dropped from the point of the buttocks should dissect the limb, passing through the point of the hock and the centre of the fetlock and foot. The importance of straightness applies just as much to the fore-leg, except that it is considered acceptable for the hocks to turn in very slightly. This makes it mechanically easier for the horse to move straight, while broad-beamed horses with absolutely straight hocks sometimes twist them out as they move and swivel their feet as they put them down. 'Cow hocks', where the hocks turn in considerably, lack power.

The position of the hock is important for strength and soundness. When the horse is standing square, the point of the hock should be in line with the point of the buttock, with the cannon bone vertical. 'Sickle hocks' with an excessive angle (the cannon bone sloping forward) lack strength, as do hocks set out behind the horse which tend to push rather than carry. An over-straight hock can indicate speed but can throw strain higher up the limb and the horse may have difficulty lowering the quarters for more advanced dressage or jumping.

The shape of the feet is very important. They

Freedom of movement, soundness and straightness are all affected by conformation. This horse and rider appear to be relaxed and comfortable.

should be round and symmetrical, ideally at an angle of about 50° to the ground, with strong wide heels and a well-developed frog. The feet should be in proportion to the size of the horse. Too small a foot will be over-stressed while big feet are ungainly and increase the chance of brushing. Above all, both front and back should make a pair. Any unevenness in size or shape could be an indication that changes are occurring within the foot which could lead to lameness *(see Chapter Three)*. Small 'boxy' feet, leaving little space for the internal structures of the foot, are less efficient at absorbing concussion and shorten the stride. Flat, open, feet are prone to bruising and, if weak-heeled, predispose all sorts of foot problems such as navicular syndrome. The balance of the foot is extremely important and, although the way the horse is shod can make or mar this, good natural conformation gives the animal a head start. The condition of the feet is equally important *(see Chapter Seven)*.

Action and movement The aim is absolutely straight action, minimizing both the stress to the limbs and the risk of the horse knocking into itself. Straight action is a high priority for showing and to a lesser extent for dressage. Conformation faults, such as crooked limbs, will lead to faulty action which can vary a lot depending on the exact make and shape of the horse. For example, one broad-chested horse may have a rolling gait and move wide while another will be base-narrow, moving close and brushing. A narrow animal will usually move close. Unless its action is perfectly straight it will often knock into itself. Horses that toe-out are prone to brushing because the flight arc of the leg moves inwards.

Good movement should always be free, elastic, and regular: but there will be variations depending on the type of horse. A fairly low 'daisy-cutting'

stride is suited to galloping and the elegant riding horse; a shorter springy one to show-jumping, and plenty of joint flexion with a good length of stride to dressage. A novice rider will be more comfortable on a less than extravagant mover. Driving horses are often prized for knee action that most riders would try to avoid!

Look at the horse's action from the front, back, and side when he is moving actively, but not too fast. Watch the way the legs move through the air and how they approach the ground. Are the feet lifted clear of the ground or the toes dragged? – a sign of stiffness and potential lameness. Are the joints well-flexed and do the limbs move forward freely with no stiffness or jerkiness and exactly evenly on both sides? He should clearly 'over-track' in walk, the hind-legs touching the ground in advance of the prints left by the fore-feet, and 'track up' (stepping into the prints) in trot. A short-legged/long-bodied horse will find this more difficult but should still bring the hind-leg well forward as he moves.

Finally, look again at the whole horse. Is he slightly plain, rather coarse or rangy, but with sound workmanlike conformation, or does he have the more chiselled features and fluid lines that are the hallmark of quality.

No horse has perfect conformation and movement. What matters is its suitability for the job in hand and the degree and significance of any faults in this context. Weighing up the pros and cons accurately takes much practice but can mean the difference between success and failure, whether hacking or competing at the highest level.

Colours

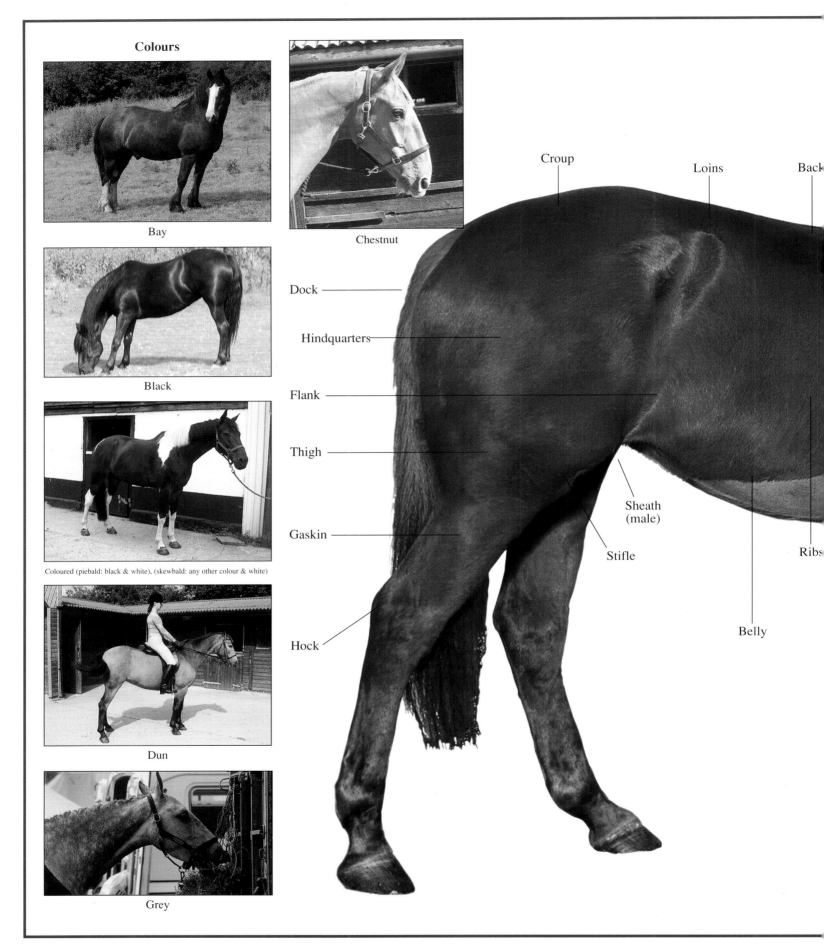

Bay

Chestnut

Black

Coloured (piebald: black & white), (skewbald: any other colour & white)

Dun

Grey

Croup

Loins

Back

Dock

Hindquarters

Flank

Thigh

Sheath (male)

Gaskin

Stifle

Ribs

Belly

Hock

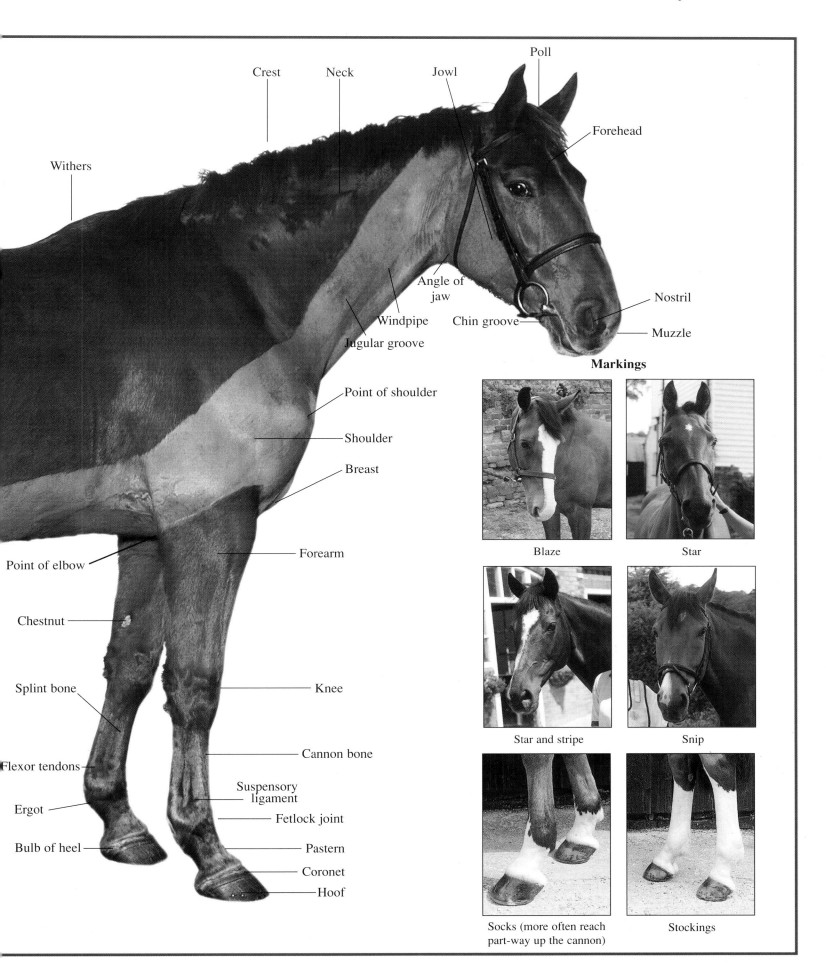

Crest

Neck

Jowl

Poll

Forehead

Withers

Angle of jaw

Nostril

Windpipe

Chin groove

Muzzle

Jugular groove

Point of shoulder

Shoulder

Breast

Forearm

Point of elbow

Chestnut

Splint bone

Knee

Cannon bone

Flexor tendons

Suspensory ligament

Ergot

Fetlock joint

Bulb of heel

Pastern

Coronet

Hoof

Markings

Blaze

Star

Star and stripe

Snip

Socks (more often reach part-way up the cannon)

Stockings

Chapter Two
CARING FOR YOUR HORSE

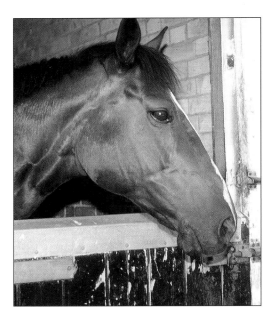

horse which is comfortable and happy in his surroundings will be easier to handle and ride and be generally more fun to be with. Horses are as individual as people: some will thrive in a busy environment where they can see what is going on while others prefer a quiet secluded yard. Nothing to look at spells boredom for some, and can lead to stable vices, while a distant view of exciting goings-on could agitate a sensitive animal. Horses often feel they own their 'patch', which includes the space outside their stable. Narrow passageways, particularly indoors, can encourage bullying which, apart from upsetting the horses, can be dangerous for their handlers who might be bitten or trampled in the rush. Even if adjoining horses are unable to touch, they can still affect the well-being of one another. A grille or window between two stables is a good idea if the occupants are friends but one will sometimes torment or bully the other, making it timid and anxious or furious at having its peace

and quiet disrupted. Low walls between indoor boxes are even worse in this respect.

The size of the individual loose box is very important. Horses can suffer from claustrophobia and a big horse that refuses to go through a low or narrow doorway is not being awkward, just afraid that he may knock his hips or bang his head. Unfortunately, two common reactions to fright are to throw up the head and run forward or back, increasing the chance of injury which he will never forget. If the stable is too small the horse is more likely to get 'cast', that is, stuck with his feet too near the wall and be unable to push off or swing over and get up. He could lie there for some time, thrashing about and possibly injuring himself as he attempts to get to his feet. More cautious animals will be reluctant to lie down or roll in the first place and will become tired and stressed as a result.

Ventilation is most important so, unless your stables are very exposed, keep the top door open

whatever the weather. A window that opens should be in the same wall as the door to prevent draughts. Extra vents in the roof and side walls are useful as wooden stables can be very hot and stuffy in summer. Taking out the top couple of boards in the back wall, or having them on hinges so that they will open, will help create a welcome through breeze in hot weather.

Stabling This usually consists of purpose-built outdoor loose boxes or an indoor American barn system: conversions of existing farm buildings can also be successful.

Loose boxes Must be of strong construction. Brick is the first choice though very expensive, followed by concrete blocks. Wooden prefabricated stabling is very popular. It is warm and, if well maintained, will last for many years. Quality is reflected in price and the more expensive are likely to last longer, being of superior timber and construction.

Wooden stables should be bolted rather than nailed together. A horse can push out wooden walls that are merely nailed together and kick through wooden and even single-brick walls. A lining of wooden kick boards, to a height of at least 1.2 m (4 ft), is essential for wooden stables. The use of 'bat straps' will hold the roof struts on securely. Make sure the stables are bolted down to the concrete base using raw bolts – stables have been known to fly away in a high wind!

Indoor stables Usually consist of two rows of stables facing inwards with a central alleyway which should be at least 4 m (12 ft) wide and preferably wider. The individual loose boxes may be of brick or steel-frame construction. Inner doors are often sliding to save space. A useful variation is to have normal stable doors on the

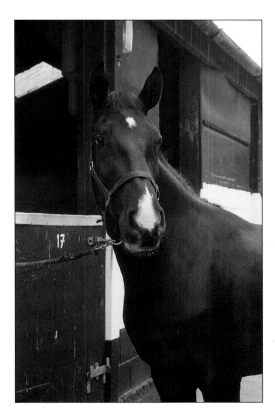

Opposite above
A stabled horse needs a well-ventilated, warm, sturdily-built stable of suitable size. Some horses thrive in a busy yard, such as a riding school, while others may appreciate a quieter environment. Observe your horse's reactions and check that he is happy in his surroundings.

Opposite below
Traditional brick stables are the best option. They are built to last, are cosy and draught-free.

Top
Wooden loose boxes are a good, cheap option for stabling horses. These have 'kick bolts' and a metal anti-chew strip on the bottom doors.

Above
An indoor stable complex showing well-built, high-quality loose boxes which are equally suited to very hot as well as cooler climates.

Left
These home-made stables, made from building blocks, are light and airy.

outside wall of each box with a narrower alleyway internally so that work can be done under cover. These offer many advantages: they are warmer in cold weather, are pleasant to work in, and offer a social environment for the horses.

The disadvantages are that fire will spread quickly, with increased smoke risk, and it will be harder to evacuate the horses. It is important that there are large double doors at either end and that they are never obstructed: in a long block there should also be doors in the middle.

Indoor stables that are poorly ventilated are less than ideal for horses with allergies to fungal spores in hay or straw and infection may spread more easily. Blocks should be constructed with as much ventilation as possible and all horses should be on dust-free bedding and forage.

Stable Management

The day-to-day care of horses consists of a number of straightforward tasks. It is the manner in which they are carried out that makes all the difference. The groom who takes time to get to know each individual animal and form a relationship with them will not only enjoy stable tasks more but be quick to notice any changes in their behaviour or physical state, good or bad. The more the horse trusts and respects the person caring for him, the easier he will be to handle when he is excited or upset.

Fire Safety Drill

Use your common sense around the stable yard. Remember that hay, straw and wooden stables are extremely flammable. Remove unnecessary fire risks and keep all exits clear. Don't smoke or light fires anywhere near the stable yard. Make sure that there are sufficient fire extinguishers, water hoses and sand and water buckets and a clear sign outlining correct procedure in case of emergency.

1) Sound fire alarm; telephone Fire Department, using the emergency number.
2) Account for all personnel (it is a wise precaution to have already initiated some form of register for signing in and out).
3) If practicable, contain and attempt to extinguish a small fire BUT
4) Evacuate people and horses first if they are in immediate danger. Lead horses out to a safe area in the open air: a coat over a horse's head will help to calm it. Prevent horses breaking loose. Start with horses nearest the fire and, in case they rush back into danger, shut stable doors afterwards.
5) It is sensible to:
   (a) Shut doors and windows once the building is completely empty.
   (b) Aim extinguishers and water at the base of the fire and spray or douse with water.
   (c) Never use water on electrical appliances – use appropriate extinguisher.
6) DIRECT FIRE-FIGHTERS TO FIRE.
7) Check horses afterwards for injury/stress.

Horses need to feel secure in their environment and thrive on routine. After physical safety, water and food are their main requirements. They get to know when these are due and eagerly await their feed at the appointed time. Irregular feed times badly affect both their digestion and mental state. It is said that European vets have to work overtime dealing with cases of colic when summer and winter time adjustments cause changes of routine, upsetting a horse's delicate equilibrium. Of course your horse's daily routine will vary according to his and your life-style just as the daily routine in a racing yard, hunting stable and riding school will each be quite different. All, however, will be conducted within a regular framework. Unfortunately, sticking to a totally rigid pattern of exercise or turn-out can present its own difficulties. Some horses become extremely agitated if for any reason their routine is altered and they are ridden when they expect to be turned out or are separated from a favourite companion who normally shares their field. They can form very strong attachments and refuse to settle when travelling alone or at a competition, frantically whinnying at any animal they think they recognize. Building their independence and teaching them to accept variations in routine takes time. Persuading an insecure horse to adopt you as his substitute friend is often the best approach.

If possible, avoid leaving one horse stabled on its own. Some will resign themselves to solitary confinement quite calmly; others will rush around

their box, kicking the walls, charging the door or trying to jump out. Vices (such as weaving) often start in this kind of situation. Apart from the obvious distress and risk of injury the horse will lose condition, may get colic, and his performance when ridden may be affected.

A horse unused to being stabled or one that has been transferred to a strange yard may initially behave in a similar way. Your presence can reassure and soothe; but if he is very upset, stay outside the box rather than risk getting kicked or knocked over. Hay and water should be put at the front of the stable but not right by the door. Buckets are easily kicked over, so remove their handles for safety's sake.

Once they have grown accustomed to their surroundings, horses should be calm and relaxed. If they are not, look for a reason and find the solution.

A practical routine

First thing in the morning, check the horse carefully. As well as inspecting his overall appearance and that of the stable this should include looking and feeling for injuries (see Chapter Three).

Give the horse some hay to get its digestion going, some fresh water and then what it has been waiting for – breakfast! All the horses should be fed at the same time. It is unnecessarily distressing for some to be made to wait while others are fed.

If for any reason you cannot give a horse a

Opposite
Different kinds of bedding are available and you will find one suitable for your horse's needs. Recycled shredded paper is becoming increasingly popular and this horse appears to be happy and comfortable with it.

Left
Depending on the type of bedding you use, various mucking-out tools will be required. Make sure they are in good repair and up to the job as old or unsuitable tools will make the task harder. Tools should always be tidied away after use, out of the reach of horses.

Below left
Tie the haynet correctly. When empty, it must be high enough to avoid the horse getting a foot stuck in the holes.

Below
Keeping the muck heap tidy is often the last job on your list. However, maintaining a tidy heap is part of keeping a stable yard spick-and-span and will make the task of mucking out less tedious.

full feed at the same time as its companions, a few handfuls in a bowl will prevent it feeling left out. Fresh water must be a priority. Leaving last night's dregs until mid-morning because the taps have frozen is unacceptable. Change the water whenever necessary and always at midday and again in the evening – never top up buckets.

After exercise and when the horse is brought in from the field check him again thoroughly – washing any mud off his legs makes this easier but can lead to soreness (*see Mud fever, page 29*).

Trot him up as he comes in from the field to make sure he is sound. In the evening, make sure you check that he has finished up his feed and is comfortable and eating hay before you leave. Ideally, do a final check, giving fresh water and hay, last thing at night. If you live away from the premises, give the bulk of the hay just before you leave so that it lasts as long as possible throughout the night.

You may wish to vary your routine according to the weather and whether it is summer or winter. In hot weather, most horses prefer to be turned out at night when flies are less bothersome. However, they will be keen to sleep rather than work when brought in in the morning!

Mucking out The horse needs a non-slip warm surface to cushion his feet when standing, and his body when lying down, and it is vital that this is properly maintained. A wet bed, smelling of ammonia, is not only extremely unpleasant but bad for the horse's feet and will affect his breathing: fungal spores occur even in clean straw and poorly mucked-out woodchip will cause breathing problems in susceptible animals. Always provide a thick bed, even if the horse is only in the stable or stall for an hour or two. Horses dislike staling onto hard surfaces where urine may splash, causing them to slip if the bedding is thin.

How to muck out If possible, remove the horse from his box and tie him up in a safe place away from tools, barrows and other horses.

If mucking out while the horse is in the stable it must be tied up – jumping wheelbarrows seems to be a favourite occupation! Be particularly careful with tools and never leave them in the box.
• Remove feed bowl/buckets/haynet.
• Daily mucking out is desirable. If time is short, a deep litter could be laid during the week as long as obvious soiled areas are removed daily and the entire litter dug out at the weekend.
• Deep-litter beds are warm and comfortable but can be smelly. Good ventilation is needed and a box with ample space. They are not suitable for horses allergic to dust and fungal spores and will need digging out every few months, which is very hard work.
• Banking the bedding up around the walls prevents draughts and makes comfortable pillows but unless very thick and high is unlikely to prevent a horse from getting cast. An anti-cast bar attached to the walls is more effective.
• Rubber matting prevents slipping and injury when lying down and cushions the horse's legs. It is excellent under a conventional bed – check on drainage requirements. It can be used on its own, though uninviting, and is very quick to muck out.
• Continue the bed up to the door to support the horse's legs where he stands for considerable periods.

Straw bedding This is the most traditional form. Remove all droppings and wet straw. Throw the remainder to two walls, sweeping half the floor each day. Disinfect regularly – special products are available to remove odours. Lay the bed and add clean straw. Try not to raise too much dust. Replace water-bucket.

Straw beds can be deep-littered. Start the bed off with a lot of straw. Remove droppings and straw that is obviously wet. Rearrange bed and add clean straw on top. It should be skipped out frequently and look like a normal bed but feel firmer. It should be completely cleaned out every couple of months.

Wood-shavings or hemp A good alternative to straw, though more expensive, these are ideal for bed-eaters and horses with a dust allergy. Remove all droppings. Throw unsoiled portions to the wall and remove any soiled and wet matter. Sweep and replace bed, forking up to the walls daily. Add clean shavings mainly to the wall area. It can be deep-littered in the same way as straw but is then not suitable for horses with allergies.

Shredded paper This is a low allergy-producing bedding but can be heavy to handle and blow about the yard. Remove wet areas and droppings. Sweep before replacing bed.

The muck heap This must be compacted downwards as far as possible when it will rot down more effectively, look better and take up less space.

Left
Horses can develop stable vices for a number of reasons, but standing in a stable for long periods may make them more susceptible. Crib-biting, shown here, can damage the teeth and affect the horse's condition.

Below
This horse has bars fitted to his stable door, preventing him from rocking from side to side (a vice known as weaving) which may affect his condition and put wear on his front legs.

Vices

These are usually the result of the way we keep and handle horses: it is the strong-minded, ultra-intelligent or sensitive animal who tends to develop problems. Horses have phenomenal memories and learn from experience as well as by imitating their dam: a bossy mare will tend to breed bossy foals and, if she distrusts people, her foals may well learn from her unless a patient and kindly approach persuades them otherwise.

Aggressive behaviour may be triggered by impatient or rough handling or by a timid groom allowing the horse to take charge.

Stable vices include kicking, biting, box-walking, rug-tearing, weaving (swaying from side to side, usually at the stable door or field gate), wind-sucking (arching the neck and gulping down air into the stomach), crib-biting (grasping an object such as the top of a door in the teeth and swallowing air in the process).

Weaving, wind-sucking, and crib-biting have previously been regarded as imitated behaviour, but recent research disputes this. They appear to develop from stress, boredom or impatience, and often show up at feed-time. Preventatives include anti-weave grilles, anti-wind-sucking straps and removing anything that the horse can grab in his teeth. Some argue that removing the horse equivalent of a cigarette or chewed finger-nails puts the horse under increased stress. Freely-given hay, more time in the field, a calmer environment or toys to play with are just some ideas that may help.

The horse at grass

Wandering in a peaceful sheltered paddock, munching at well-maintained pasture in the company of friends, is for most horses pure bliss.

We can't all have palatial paddocks but the advantages of having even a small area for turn-out cannot be over-emphasized. Although horses can certainly be kept fit and healthy when stabled all the time, they undoubtedly enjoy a more natural environment and the freedom to kick up their heels, socialize and relax.

The chance to unwind is important to any hard-working horse, both on a daily basis and at the end of a busy season. Many highly-strung horses become almost unmanageable without a daily spell at grass. Young stock, of course, needs space to move, develop and learn about life, while for older horses the chance to gently move about helps loosen stiff joints.

Grass is a cheap feed, relatively speaking, and can provide valuable 'keep' as part or all of the daily ration depending on the situation and time of year.

There is nothing better than good grass for mares, foals and young stock or for bringing an ailing animal to better condition. 'Good' grass means suitable for the type of horse or pony and the job it has to do. Having ample supplies of grass can be a mixed blessing as the type of rich pasture suitable for Thoroughbreds could literally 'kill with kindness' a small native pony. Rich spring grass will make some horses suddenly over-excited, as though they were being fed oats, and there is the ever-present danger of laminitis, particularly in fat animals and ponies.

Too little grass is unfortunately an all-too-common sight with ever-increasing areas of rank long grass and weeds soured by horses' droppings. Horses will avoid grazing these areas if at all possible, preferring to eat the remaining pasture almost bare. They may also lean through fences to get to grass outside, stretching wire and loosening posts. Hungry horses will start to chew tree-bark,

eventually killing the tree, and may resort to eating poisonous weeds that they would normally avoid. They will also tend to both play and argue more, especially when hanging around the gate waiting to be brought in or fed. All these activities are likely to lead to injuries, be they kicks, cuts from wires, worm infestation *(see Parasitic Worms, page 32)*, or poisoning.

It is important to check the field daily. Ensure that fencing is secure, gates are in good repair, and that there are no poisonous plants, potholes or rubbish. Pick up droppings, ideally every day, especially if the paddock is small. Check that there is sufficient clean water on hand as well as shelter.

Caring for the horse at grass In theory, any horse can live at grass. Native ponies positively prefer the outdoor life and most others, even Thoroughbreds, cope very well if given sheltered, well-drained conditions and sufficient food. In fact, the field shelter will probably be used most in summer as a refuge from the flies which seem to particularly plague thin-skinned types. Your own forethought and powers of observation are the key factors in ensuring the welfare of your horse. Keep a careful eye on his condition, feeling through his long coat in winter and noticing the extra plumpness and hardened crest which can precede laminitis in summer. If your horse starts to lose condition in winter, and you are already feeding him plenty, he may be telling you that he cannot manage to work and maintain his condition or that he is unable to cope at all and needs to come into a warm stable at night. Also notice if he seems content in both his expression and behaviour.

This may be the horse's natural environment but even a hairy pony should never be stuck in a field and left to its own devices. Check your horse morning and evening – try to keep to regular times

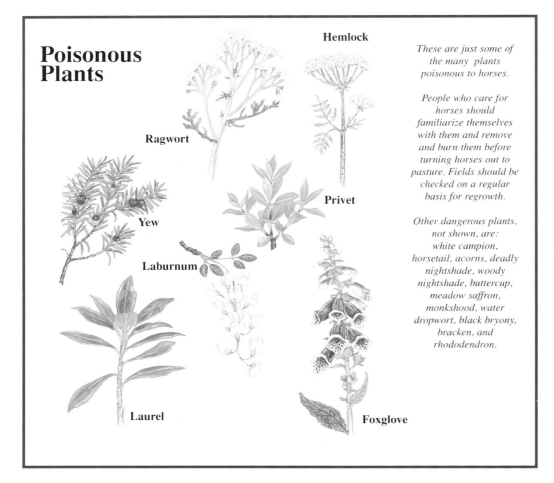

Poisonous Plants

Hemlock

Ragwort

Yew

Laburnum

Privet

Laurel

Foxglove

These are just some of the many plants poisonous to horses.

People who care for horses should familiarize themselves with them and remove and burn them before turning horses out to pasture. Fields should be checked on a regular basis for regrowth.

Other dangerous plants, not shown, are: white campion, horsetail, acorns, deadly nightshade, woody nightshade, buttercup, meadow saffron, monkshood, water dropwort, black bryony, bracken, and rhododendron.

– and develop a relationship with him so that he looks forward to seeing you and enjoys being caught to have his rug adjusted, being groomed, fussed over and fed. Make up a feed of carrots and apples if he doesn't need a proper feed. He will then be much easier to catch and you may be able to teach him to come to call. Make sure your grooming is suitable for a grass-kept horse *(see Grooming horses at grass, page 25)*. It helps if there is a stable into which he can be brought. If this is not possible, a small fenced-off area will enable him to be handled and fed away from other loose horses.

Try to allow an hour off the grass before you ride or stick to walking until the hour is up. You should try to bring your horse home cool and relaxed by walking the last 10 or 20 minutes. He may, however, still be sweating if he has worked hard or has a full winter coat, or he may be wet from rain. In warm weather it is fine to wash off the sweat, removing excess water with a scraper or towel before turning him out. If it is cold, and he wears a New Zealand rug, rub him down with straw or towels and leave him 'thatched' or wearing a cooler rug in a stable or at least out of the wind until he is as dry as possible *(see Grooming, page 24)*. Walk him round if he seems cold. An alternative would be to rub him down and then turn him out in one New Zealand, returning a couple of hours later to replace the damp rug with a spare one.

If the horse has a long coat and is not

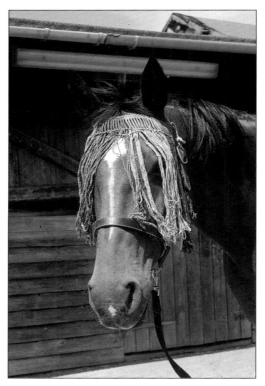

In summer, a fly fringe can help reduce the burden of flies a horse has to bear. Use a leather headcollar or a special type which will easily break if the horse gets caught up.

normally rugged, it may be preferable to put him straight out in the field where he can move around and keep warm. It is best not to rub him down as you will make the whole coat damp; his undercoat is probably still dry, even if he is quite wet on top. It should go without saying that you should avoid letting a grass-kept horse get too sweated up in the first place.

Horses and ponies at grass 24 hours a day can work steadily without problems but it would be unfair to expect a horse in 'soft' condition with a 'grass belly' to work hard or fast. Unfortunately this frequently happens each spring and summer when unsuspecting little fat ponies who have been doing nothing more than eat and sleep are suddenly removed from the field and expected to jump and perform at gymkhanas and pony club meetings with great vigour and very little preparation.

It is most important that you check your horse twice daily. Make sure that he is behaving normally with his companions, grazing, mutually grooming and fly-swatting, occasionally rolling, playing and sleeping. Check that he is sound at walk and trot; look him over carefully for wounds and feel for any swellings, assessing his general condition at the same time.

Look out for signs that all is not well: repeated agitated rolling, lying down with reluctance to get up, standing alone, and being generally unsettled in his behaviour. He could be suffering from lameness, cold, insect irritation, hunger, thirst, or bullying, or there may well be other outside influences which have frightened or excited him.

In summer it is most important that he is sufficiently protected from flies, midges and horse-flies which can cause painful swellings, watery infected eyes, and in severe cases, sweet-itch. Douse him regularly with insect repellent and remove any eggs which have been laid on legs and belly.

Watch out for sunburn and allergies and – when the grass is rich and plentiful – laminitis.

In winter, check that he is warm and moving around enough; check that his rug is dry underneath and hasn't caused any rubs. It is very important that you check feet and legs for mud fever, cracked heels, thrush, bruises and abscesses in the feet and examine the state of his shoes. Also watch out for rain-scald, lice and sore runny eyes. Always keep an eye on the weather and treat him accordingly.

Fencing It is vital that your horse's field is properly fenced. The fence should be at least 1.2 m (4 ft) high with the bottom rail or wire at least 38 cm (15 inches) off the ground. There are many types of fencing available. Post and rail is smart and safe, though an expensive option, but if properly built and treated with creosote to prevent horses from chewing it, will last many years and is easy to repair.

There are a variety of flexible synthetic rails on the market which are durable and safe.

A well-maintained hedge is an excellent

Left
Hedges are a traditional form of barrier and provide shelter from strong winds. They need to be regularly checked and maintained.

choice. It should be as thick as possible, at least 1.2 m (4 ft) wide, composed of a non-poisonous plant, with no gaps likely to appear in winter. Any gaps should be filled with post and rail or a line of electric fencing a few feet inside the hedge.

Plain wire is also an acceptable form of fencing but is best topped with a solid rail which will make it more visible to horses. It is a lot cheaper than post and rail but horses do tend to push through it and can get their legs caught in the wire, leading to serious injury.

Electric fencing runs from a battery or off the mains with a transformer. It consists of plastic stakes threaded with tape through which the current passes. Horses must be shown its effect by touching their noses to it. It is used for temporary fencing to allow strip grazing to rest sections of a field: it can also be used to reinforce existing fencing such as hedges. There is also available a far sturdier version for permanent fencing.

Heavy-duty wire mesh, which is stock-proof, is also an option and cheaper that stud rail. Once again, it is best topped with a rail to make it more visible. It can be dangerous, however, particularly for ponies and foals who may get their feet entangled.

Avoid barbed wire if you possibly can. It is

Left
Post and rail fencing, though expensive, is a good safe option.

Below left
Electric fencing is useful for dividing fields temporarily, especially where grazing is in short supply.

Below
An example of poor fencing, composed of barbed wire, string, and rusty old metal: to be avoided at all costs.

Above
A well-designed water trough with ball-cock mechanism which allows self-filling. The water level and state of cleanliness should be checked twice daily, especially in hot weather. Leaves from the hedge may collect in this particular trough.

Above
Security is becoming increasingly important and it is comforting to know that your field is safe. Use a strong lock and chain on gates and check fences regularly.

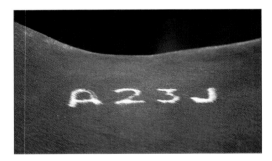

Above
Many horses are stolen every year, causing grief to their owners. It is a good idea to have your horse freeze-branded, which is painless. Each personal number is lodged with an international data base to prevent your horse being sold on without your permission.

an inexpensive option but can cause serious injuries. It is safer if the bottom strand is plain wire. It is very dangerous in fields dividing horses from one another.

Avoid using wire netting, sheep or pig wire, chestnut fencing or metal park rails: these are all highly dangerous to horses.

Water supply It is important that the field has a constant water supply. The best option is a galvanized or polyethylene trough with an integral protected ball-cock mechanism, with no sharp or

protruding edges and a drain hole set on brick or concrete supports with pipes laid underground to avoid freezing in winter. The trough should be easily accessible to both horse and owner, avoiding corners, proximity to a gate, or sited beneath trees or bushes.

Any temporary containers, e.g. bins or buckets, should be secured to prevent them from tipping over and their handles removed. Water should be checked twice daily for quality and cleanliness and ice broken and removed in winter.

Streams should be checked for pollution and safety of approach. Unsuitable water supplies, such as ponds, should be fenced off.

Gates An ideal gate should be 3 m (10 ft) or preferably 3.75 m (12 ft) wide to allow machinery and vehicles to pass through. It must be as high as the fences. Protruding latches are a potential hazard.

Choose a gate in which horses cannot get their feet caught. Do not site near corners of fields where horses and people can be cornered and kicked when entering or leaving.

Shelter It is important that your field is equipped with adequate shelter from wind, rain and snow, hot sun and flies. A robust field shelter is ideal; it must be carefully positioned and large enough to avoid animals becoming trapped. However, natural windbreaks such as thick hedges, stone walls and dips in the ground are all useful. Large trees are good for protection against sun and flies.

Life in the field By observing horses in a field you will learn a lot about their individual personalities. You will notice how they resolve differences and assert their authority in an unmistakable manner, be it by body language or with a bite or kick before generally settling back

to grazing or dozing as before.

Horses are herd animals and are happiest in a group. They will always sort themselves into a pecking order and once this is settled co-exist happily. Arguments may be caused by individual members gaining in confidence and attempting to move up the order, or by outside influences such as being fed titbits over the fence.

Few horses are really aggressive: most injuries result from play or minor squabbles, metal shoes inflicting far greater injury than was intended. Sometimes one horse will take a particular dislike to another and make its life a misery, bullying it, hassling it constantly, and never allowing it any rest. Should you encounter a really unpleasant animal, liable to chase or corner another, and it is really intent on causing injury, then separate it from other horses immediately. Waiting to see if they will sort out their own differences is asking for a hefty vet's bill or worse.

Horses are as varied as people. There are the self-contained loners, the calm, friendly types who get on with everyone, the assertive ones who are always in charge (often mares) and the playful types who never seem to know when to stop and are always getting injured. Some have a well developed instinct for self-preservation while others blunder into every kind of trouble. Some old horses still love to play but most would prefer not to be pestered by youngsters. Try, if you can,

Below
A purpose-built field shelter is ideal for horses at grass who require protection from wind and rain in winter and shade and safeguard from flies in summer. The opening must be large enough to prevent horses being trapped in corners by bullies and must face away from the prevailing wind.

him to the group, preferably beginning with the quiet, friendly ones. It is a good idea to put on brushing-boots and knee-boots are also a wise precaution though should not be left on too long as they may cause rubbing.

Feeding horses in the field Don't short-feed horses in the field; always remove the horse, preferably out of sight of others which are still out. Carrying bowls of food into a field puts you at risk of being caught in the middle of a fight.

In winter it will be necessary to feed hay twice a day. Spread it on as dry an area as possible to prevent it being churned into the mud. Movable hay racks can be useful where there are a small number of animals who get on well together. Use at least two more heaps of hay than there are numbers of animals to allow the ones at the bottom of the pecking order to get their fair share. If only a few horses are sharing a field shelter, putting hay in a manger may work, but can lead to bullying and some may miss out.

Left
These horses in Wyoming, U.S.A. are well prepared for wintry conditions with warm, well-fitting New Zealand rugs. When temperatures plunge you will need to check horses very regularly and extra feed will be necessary to provide them with sufficient energy to keep warm.

Below
Catching a horse which does not particularly wish to be caught requires tact and experience.

to divide them into compatible groups. Is the timid gelding always by himself by choice or has he been elbowed out?

Sometimes mini-herds develop within the main group, one horse taking a fancy to one or more of the others and guarding them jealously from the rest. This happens rather more often in groups where there are both males and females.

Many yards insist that mares and geldings are turned out in separate fields. This is a wise precaution, especially in large yards, reducing disagreements and injuries. Much depends on the individual animal. Some mares are incredibly flirty when in season, chatting up the boys but at the same time kicking out at an ill-timed advance. Equally, some geldings seem all too aware of what they are missing and may pester the mares or fight over them. However, there are plenty of mares and geldings who live together happily as brothers and sisters. Grazing any horses (particularly mares and geldings) in adjoining fields can be problematical, especially if they can touch one another. Horses introduce themselves to one another by blowing and sniffing nose to nose. Depending on the conversation there may be an affronted squeal and involuntary striking out with a front leg. Pawing at the fence and lashing out with the hind-legs may also cause self-inflicted injuries and bold or clumsy types may jump or barge straight through.

Turning horses out together is to automatically risk injury but is in most cases the only practical way and the happiest situation for all concerned. Very valuable or accident-prone animals are best with one quiet companion or left alone in sight of other horses if they will settle happily. It goes without saying that high, safe fencing is essential. Even fit horses can generally be safely turned out for an hour or two on a daily basis if this is a regular occurrence. However, a sudden decision to give a fit stable-kept horse some time in the field is a recipe for disaster.

Introducing a new horse into the group Start off by introducing the newcomer to one quiet, friendly horse that is good at avoiding trouble. Ideally, do this in a field adjoining the group but with safe double fencing so that he can see but not touch. There may be a risk that the horse may jump, so watch him carefully.

After one or two weeks of this, introduce

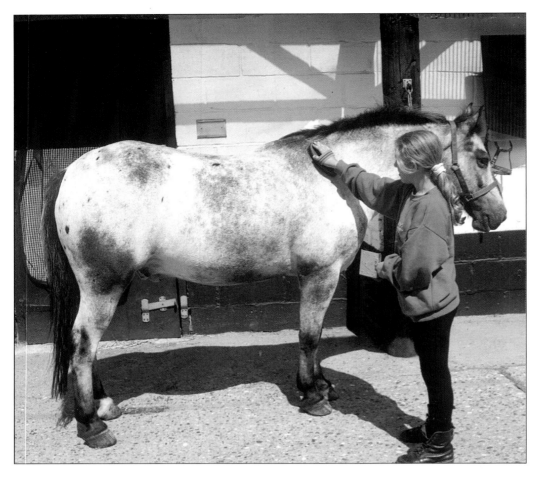

After work Sponge off and, using a sweat scraper, remove excess water or towel dry. Pick out feet and check shoes (check for injuries). When dry, brush off any mud or sweat residues.

Picking out the feet Pick out all four feet in the same order daily – your horse will become accustomed to the routine and will pick up his feet for you. Use downward strokes of the hoof pick to remove the muck and make use of the situation to check for health and the condition of the shoe.

Grooming

Grooming is an important part of a horse's care and well-being. It improves his appearance, cleans his coat, improves the elimination of waste products through the skin and makes him more comfortable, reducing the incidence of skin disease. It aids circulation and the massaging effect contributes to muscle development and tone.

Horses should always be groomed before riding to prevent tack from rubbing and is a good opportunity to check for injuries and insect bites. Feel with your hand while brushing.

The Stabled Horse
Quartering This is usually done first thing in the morning before exercise. Fold the rugs either back or forwards, but avoid completely removing them. Brush over quickly and remove stable stains. Pick out the feet and check shoes for looseness or wear. Brush and tidy mane and tail and clean the eyes and nose.

Strapping This is a thorough grooming after exercise when the pores are open – the horse must be dry. Remove all sweat, mud and dirt using a dandy brush. Then give him a thorough body brush finishing up by removing any excess dust with a damp stable rubber. Brush and 'lay' the mane and tail, wipe the eyes and nose and under the dock. First or last thing, pick out the feet and check the shoes. Last of all, oil the feet – hoof oil improves appearance but is not always good for the feet, so ask your farrier before using it daily.

Dandy brush and rubber curry Only use the rubber curry for the removal of excess dry mud and hair. This tool is particularly useful when the horse is changing his coat. The dandy brush is very hard and should be used with care (do not use on the head).

Body brushing This deep-cleans the coat and skin, removing scurf and excess grease and distributing natural oils throughout the hair. It has a massaging effect and improves the blood supply and muscle tone. Only use the metal curry comb for cleaning the body brush. Use downward strokes to avoid cutting yourself on the teeth.

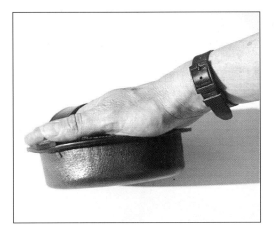

Wisping (also called strapping) This massages the large muscle groups of the neck, shoulders and hindquarters using a hay wisp or leather pad. Never wisp over bony areas, back, loins or head. It is intended to aid muscle development and put a

gloss on the coat as well as developing the crest or quarters, improving appearance. However, some doubt its benefits.

Initially untie the horse to avoid upsetting it, when it could well pull back, and start with the forehand. Begin gently, building up to short, firm, rhythmical strokes for a maximum of 10 minutes. Be firm but tactful, especially when grooming the head and around the ticklish areas of abdomen, loins and between the back legs. Avoid using a dandy brush on a clipped horse. You should groom and wisp using the hand nearest the horse, i.e. left hand, left side; this is more effective as well as evening up the groom's muscles!

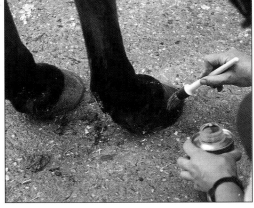

Oiling the feet When working close to the horse's legs or feet, such as when oiling the feet, make sure you crouch well clear of the horse's legs and stay to the side of it rather than in front of the feet. Never kneel.

Brushing the tail Groom the tail with the body brush to avoid breaking the hairs. You can separate any tangles with your fingers. Stand close to the horse and to the side to avoid the possibility of being kicked.

Washing the eyes This should be done gently with clean water and cotton wool.

Grooming horses at grass Generally avoid body brushing as this removes grease needed for warmth and waterproofing. Before work, pick out the feet, check the shoes and for injuries. Remove dry mud, paying special attention to areas that will be covered by tack. Do not brush wet mud. Tidy the mane and tail (in winter a light coating of vegetable oil or liquid paraffin will prevent mud from sticking). Sponge the eyes and nose.

After work, always aim to return the horse cool to his stable and, if possible, dry. In summer it is a good idea to sponge off excess sweat.

Washing Horses

On a hot summer's day, or before a show, your horse will benefit from a good wash which he will greatly enjoy. Choose a surface where water can easily drain away and a location out of the wind.

Wet the horse with a hose or sponge (tactfully!). Use warm water, if possible, especially for the tail area. Then massage in dilute horse shampoo. Rinse carefully and remove surplus water with a sweat scraper. Make sure you clean to the roots of mane and tail. Put the end of the tail in a bucket to wash it. With a docile horse you can twirl the hair around to remove excess water. Note that if you wash the mane and tail the day before you plait it, it will be very slippery! Dry the horse with towels and put on a cooler or anti-sweat rug if the weather is at all cold. On a warm day, stand him in the sun, and walk or lunge him until he is dry; if you put him in his stable he will roll straightaway! Don't let him chill when he will end up stiff and uncomfortable.

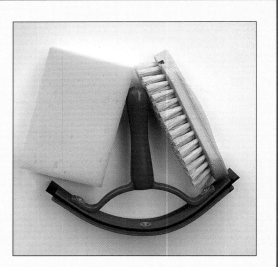

Right
A sponge, water brush and sweat scraper are the useful tools you will need when hosing down your horse.

Below
In hot weather, after strenuous work, your horse will appreciate being hosed down. Initially apply the hose low down on the horse's front legs, working your way up to avoid a sudden contrast in temperature.

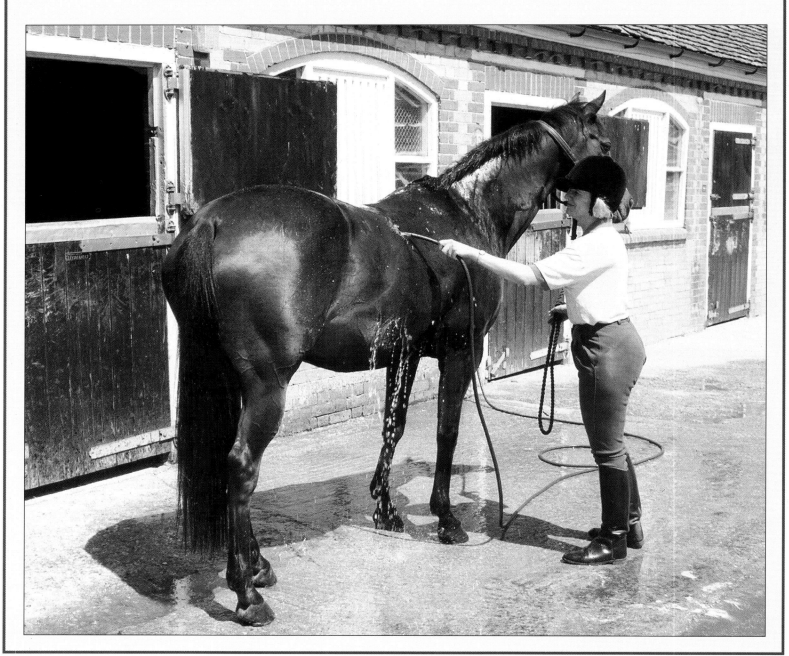

Page 24 above left
Regular grooming of the stabled horse or pony will greatly improve the appearance and protective qualities of his coat and he will enjoy it into the bargain.

Above
Turning a horse out to a high standard is an art and is an important part of the showing enthusiast's life. This immaculately groomed horse and rider are competing in a hack class.

Page 24 below right
Equip yourself with the full range of grooming tools shown here.

Chapter Three
COMMON AILMENTS AND FIRST AID

Keeping your horse healthy depends on good stable management, common sense and keen observation. Preventative medicine is vital, e.g. vaccinations for equine influenza and also tetanus, which can enter the body through the tiniest cut and usually kills. Regular worming and teeth-rasping are also essential.

A healthy horse should be alert, bright-eyed, glossy-coated, sound, and behaving in his usual way. If he becomes nervy, restless, uncharacteristically quiet or bad-tempered, he may be ill. Check him carefully morning and evening and before and after work for signs of sickness or injury (feel as well as look, especially at his legs). Make sure he is moving freely and is sound. A staring rough coat could mean he is cold or ill (check his ears are warm): mucus membranes should be salmon pink in colour. Look for water or feed not finished up. Is the bedding dishevelled or too clean. Picking up on early signs may prevent serious problems from developing. For example, too few droppings, which are firmer than usual, may be a precursor of impacted colic (blockage). Slight heat and swelling could indicate infection developing from a hidden wound or embedded thorn and, if over the tendons, is a warning to avoid fast work.

Working a horse hard when he is sickening for an illness is likely to make it far worse: if he appears to be even slightly off-colour, check his temperature, pulse and respiration and give him only easy work to do. These checks are especially important before long journeys and competitions. You may well know your horse better than anyone else, so trust your own instincts. Practise your first aid skills and get the horse used to all the procedures before you need to use them in an emergency. Get to know each horse's normal temperature, pulse and respiration rate at rest and make sure of your own proficiency in taking them. If the horse is agitated, wear your hard hat, get a responsible helper, and make sure your reactions are fast. Be calm, reassuring and patient. Above all, remember that your own safety is paramount.

Medical records should be kept of every horse in the yard. All drugs must be carefully labelled and locked away and first aid equipment readily available.

Wounds

Many wounds, if not too serious, can be treated without the help of a vet, but if there is any doubt, call him immediately. If necessary, apply direct pressure to stop bleeding. Remember, arterial bleeding (bright red and spurting) and profuse venous bleeding can be life-threatening. Thorough washing is essential. Hosing is useful for bruising and the initial cleansing of dirty wounds. Use dilute antiseptic and cotton wool, never sponges. Trim hair around the wound, if necessary. Small wounds can be left uncovered and an application of powder, cream or spray applied two to three times a day. For larger wounds, apply antibiotic cream, a non-stick dressing, clean wadding (e.g. gamgee) and bandage. Renew if dressing seems wet or has slipped and every two to three days or on your vet's advice. Remove old cream and dirt first. Check increased swelling does not cause the bandage to tighten uncomfortably. Poulticing is used for drawing bruised or infected wounds. **Call the vet immediately** if the horse's tetanus immunization is not up to date or if there is severe bleeding; he appears to be in shock and lacks

Above
A common site for wounds in horses, caused either by barbed wire or over-reaching.

Left
You will soon become accustomed to assessing your horse's general health. A bright, alert, happy look indicates he is well. Look out for warning signs of ill-health. At rest, the horse's breathing rate should be 8–12 per minute. Count each breath in and out as one (watch the flanks or the nostrils).

energy (with irregular breathing); has cold ears, a vacant stare or is reacting violently; is very lame, there is severe and increasing swelling or he has loss of feeling below the wound.

When stitching is indicated call the vet (stitching generally needs to be done within 6 hours) if the wound is deep and more than 2.5-cm (1-inch) long or there is a large downward-hanging flap of flesh.

Puncture wounds Can look small superficially but may have penetrated deeply. Deep wounds near joints and tendons and eye, mouth, and jaw injuries need immediate attention and antibiotics. Call the vet if the wound becomes infected (inflamed and producing pus), refuses to heal, develops proud flesh (formation of lumpy red tissue) or the horse is still lame.

Dressings For small wounds, dust with antibiotic wound powder or use an antibiotic spray. Use ointment to keep the wound supple and a light covering replaced two to three times a day. Remove any surplus powder/cream. For larger, clean wounds, use antibiotic powder or cream and cover with a non-adhesive dressing, gamgee tissue and a bandage to hold the wound edges together: check which direction is most effective. In the case of a leg injury, use a support bandage with padding on the opposite leg.

Dirty or infected wounds Poultice until no more pus appears, usually two to three days. Use anti-bacterial cream on wounds in areas difficult to poultice (this will draw out dirt and infection). Poulticing for too long can be counter-productive, delaying healing. Poultices should not be used on puncture wounds near joints – check with your vet. (*See also page 34.*)

Respiratory Problems

Chronic Obstructive Pulmonary Disease (COPD) or allergy to dust. The horse becomes sensitive to the spores, fungi and moulds in hay and straw and sometimes to pollen. This can be triggered by a dusty, dirty environment or be a sequel to an infection. The breathing becomes laboured and faster than usual, often with a nasal discharge and harsh dry cough. There is loss of performance, particularly at faster paces.

Coughs, colds and flu These are caused by viruses or bacteria and vaccination for equine influenza will prevent or greatly lessen the symptoms. The horse may have increased temperature, swollen throat glands, cough and nasal discharge, weakness, stiffness, loss of appetite and depression. A secondary infection may produce a thick and yellowish nasal discharge.

Strangles This is a contagious disease which lasts several weeks. The symptoms are a high temperature, listlessness, loss of appetite and depression. The horse will have a nasal discharge which becomes thick and yellow. The lymph glands between the jaws and behind the jaw below the ears become hot and swollen. The horse will have difficulty in swallowing due to abscesses and may cough. These burst after several days (up to ten) when the horse begins to recover.

Skin Problems

If your horse develops scabs or itchy areas, treat as contagious and isolate as a precaution until the vet has made his diagnosis.

Mud fever This is caused by an organism in the soil which penetrates the superficial skin layers when the skin is soggy and wet or muddy. Mainly the lower legs are affected, but sometimes also the upper legs and belly. The symptoms are scabs, often oozing, with inflammation and soreness.

Rain Scald This is caused by the same organisms as mud fever and usually occurs when the horse has been standing out in torrential rain or under dripping trees.

Mud fever usually occurs in winter but can also develop in wet summers. It is caused by an organism in the soil and develops in wet muddy conditions.

Ringworm Is caused by a fungus spread by spores that can live for months or even years. It is spread by direct contact or from infected bedding, rugs, grooming kits, tack, human clothing, the wood of stables or fencing, rats or mice. Human beings can catch it too. Usually there will be small round lesions forming grey scales or crusts with the hairs broken off just above the skin. The disease often starts on the forehead, face, neck or root of the tail and can spread to any part of the body, especially where there has been contact with the carrier, e.g. girth and saddle area. New patches usually extend from the centre outwards, hence 'ring' worm. The condition may cause itching.

Sweet Itch Takes the form of intense irritation of the mane area and base of the tail. The skin becomes thickened, swollen and scaly. In severe cases the whole of the mane and top of the tail becomes bald and the skin will redden and ooze a clear yellowish fluid. This is a disease of summertime, caused by an allergic reaction to specific midges.

Girth/Saddle Galls These often occur on unfit horses in 'soft condition' or due to dirty, stiff or badly-fitting tack. They can be caused by girths that are too loose or too tight. In mild cases the hair will be rubbed and there will be tenderness and swelling.

Lice These are tiny brownish parasites which attach their eggs to the hairs especially of the mane and top of the tail. They usually manifest themselves on animals in poor condition, especially with long coats, and more often in the winter. They spread rapidly from horse to horse. The lice suck the blood, bite and cause irritation, dragging the horse down and making him 'feel lousy'. The horse will be itchy and have rub patches on his head and neck and possibly all over. The lice and nits (eggs) should be visible but are easily missed. They have a life-cycle of approximately three weeks.

Urticaria (nettle rash) Round swellings or raised irregular patches, often with no irritation or discomfort, caused by allergic reaction to something eaten. Fly bites may cause similar reaction but will be painful.

Colic The horse has a small stomach and cannot vomit and the intestines are prone to inflammation and blockage which can be triggered by worm damage, errors or sudden changes in diet, bolting the feed, lack of water, being worked after feeding, sharp teeth, wind-sucking/crib-biting, nervous excitement, poisons or hormonal problems, e.g. when a mare is in season. The symptoms are lack of appetite, looking towards flanks, pawing the ground, kicking at the stomach, getting up and down, lying on back or sitting on haunches like a dog, rolling, straddled limbs, trying to pass water and uneasy behaviour. The pulse and temperature rates may rise due to pain as may the breathing rate.

First Aid for Colic

1. Call the vet at once and report. He will decide if an immediate visit is necessary. Prompt treatment can make all the difference.
2. Remove feed, leaving fresh water unless advised otherwise by your vet.
3. Keep the bed well banked and remove any obstructions.
4. Apply light rugs and bandages if the horse is cold or is suffering from patchy sweating.
5. Prevent violent rolling, remembering that the safety of the handler is paramount. Gentle walking may ease the pain and discourage the horse from rolling, but avoid exhausting him. Violent rolling may cause a horse to twist its gut, but is more often a sign that the gut is twisted already.
6. Check pulse/temperature/respiration and all symptoms at regular intervals (at least hourly) and report to the vet if there is any sign of worsening.

Once the horse seems better, see if it will pick at a little grass or hay. If it will, a sloppy bran mash may be fed, on the vet's advice. This will usually be about two hours after the symptoms subside. Try to ascertain and remove the cause and re-introduce small quantities of short feed over the next few days. It is likely that the horse will be suffering from dehydration after a colic attack: add electrolytes to drinking water or give by syringe to help redress the fluid imbalance. Recommence work gradually, avoiding stress.

Azoturia Generally occurs after enforced rest of as little as one day on a full concentrate diet. Slight 'tying up' symptoms may occur in fit horses working on full rations, possibly due to an electrolyte or mineral imbalance. The symptoms will usually start within 20 minutes of starting work but may occasionally appear up to several hours later. Initially, there will be a slight stiffening of the hindquarters and lameness behind. If exercise is continued, the horse will increasingly worsen and be reluctant to move. He will have painful, hard, tense muscles (usually of the loins and hindquarters). There will be sweating, restlessness, rapid pulse and respiration, raised temperature, blowing and difficulty in passing urine which may be port-coloured. In severe cases the horse may collapse. **Stop exercise at once, keep the horse warm, and call the vet.**

Lameness (Examination for)

Checking a horse for soundness calls for

Rolling and playing is part of field life; however, repeated rolling is a sign of colic which can be caused by redworm infestation among other things.

experience and precision of judgment. However, there are certain things you can do to make an assessment of our own horse if you suspect that he may be unsound.

Before trotting and walking up even takes place, take time to look at the horse in the stable. Note his stance and freedom of movement. A rested fore-leg or a constantly rested hind could be an early sign of lameness.)

Put on the headcollar or bridle. As you lead the horse out of the stable, note how he walks. It is quite common for lameness to show itself after a rest period and for the horse to loosen up when exercised.

Choose a hard, level surface. Have the horse walked away for 18 m (60 ft), and trotted back past you. Make sure the rope is kept loose so that you can assess the movement of the head and neck. Check that the horse moves in a straight line and that all four soles of his feet are clearly visible. Look out for one leg taking a shorter stride or a short, unsteady gait. As the horse trots away from you, check for even flexion of the hocks. Check for dragging toes and for one leg swinging out or too far under the body. If the horse is lame behind, the hip will generally sink on the sound side and be lifted on the lame side but may lift and fall on the lame side.

From a side view, check to see if the horse is tracking up. The horse may nod his head if lame in front and also if very lame behind. His head will lift up as the lame leg comes to the ground.

There are extra tests which will show up problems. An 8–10-m (30–32-ft) circle in hand in trot on a hard surface will reveal most cases of lameness. The horse can be turned tightly. Check to see if the hind-legs cross freely. Is there reluctance or stiffness when backed up?

Lameness on soft going may denote tendon or other soft tissue strain. Lameness on stony ground or downhill suggests foot problems. Uphill work will reveal shoulder problems.

Lameness often increases when the horse is ridden but it could be that the horse has muscular or back problems or that tack is ill-fitting. Once the lame leg has been located, check carefully for pain, heat and swelling, starting at the foot.

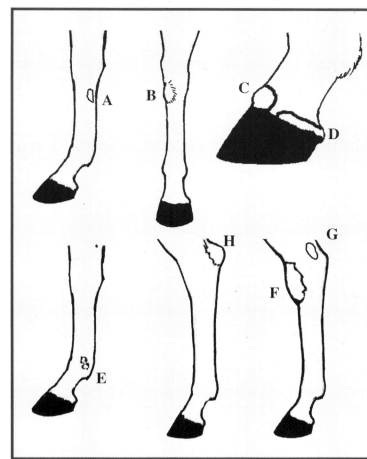

Possible causes of lameness

Bony Growths

A. Splint These usually develop where the ligaments bind the splint bone to the cannon. Initially they can be painful, but rarely cause problems once formed.

B. Bone spavin This is an arthritic condition affecting the hock and causing lameness which initially tends to wear off with exercise. The end stage of the disease is that the bones fuse completely.

C. Ringbone This is another arthritic condition of the joints between the bones of the pastern and the foot, usually causing chronic lameness. 'High' ringbone is pictured here with 'low' ringbone bulges at the coronary band.

D. Sidebone This is calcification of the lateral cartilage. It may cause lameness or an uneven gait.

Bursal Enlargements

These are usually a sign of stress or wear and tear to the joints, although they do not necessarily cause lameness.

E. Windgalls These small swellings appear on either side of the fetlock joints.

F. Bog spavin This forms on the inside front of the hock. It is soft and painless.

G. Thoroughpin This is a distension of the tendon sheath. The swelling protrudes either side of the hock.

H. Capped hock The usual cause of this is insufficient bedding, or the horse kicking a wall. There will be a fluid-filled swelling and sometimes thickened skin with initial tenderness. Capped elbow is similar and caused by friction of the heel of the shoe when the horse is lying down.

Swollen limbs may simply indicate poor circulation but could well be a sign of more serious problems. Swellings, accompanied by heat and tenderness, which do not leave an impression when pressed, are likely to be caused by infection or strain.

Strained tendons The symptoms vary according to the severity of the strain. Most severe 'breakdowns' are preceded by previous less serious damage which has not completely healed; slight symptoms should never be ignored.

Below
This horse has a chronic tendon injury and is now in retirement. The tendon has become bowed due to the build-up of scar tissue.

Below left
Older horses, with poor circulation, often get filled or oedematous legs. Standing in a stable for long periods should be avoided; when stabled, however, bandages can be applied to alleviate the problem. This horse has pronounced windgalls.

In a mild case there will be slight heat and swelling over the tendon (which may reduce on exercise) and discomfort when the tendon is palpated with the leg raised. The horse will not necessarily be lame. In a more serious case there will be heat, swelling, pain and the heel may possibly be raised from the ground with the knee forward. This will develop within a few hours of the injury.

Old, chronic injuries will result in permanently thickened and/or bowed tendons, cold and firm to the touch as a result of scar tissue, due to one bad injury or the build-up of neglected slight sprains.

The first 48 hours are critical. If the inflammatory response is not controlled, congestion occurs, the damage may worsen and healing will be delayed.

Lymphangitis Dramatic swelling of one or possibly both hind-legs occurs due to an accumulation of lymphatic fluid in the tissues. There is often a characteristic ridge at the level of the stifle and the surface lymph vessels and nodes may be prominent. The leg will be hot and painful, fluid may escape through the skin, and the horse may have a slightly raised temperature. The horse will be reluctant to walk or may not be able to take weight on the leg. Lymphangitis is usually due to an infection, probably from an old wound (not necessarily a large one) spreading to the lymphatic system. It may also be caused by excessive feeding and insufficient exercise.

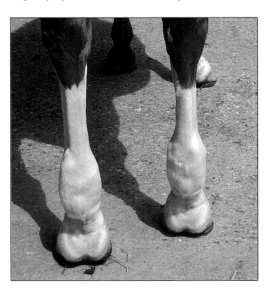

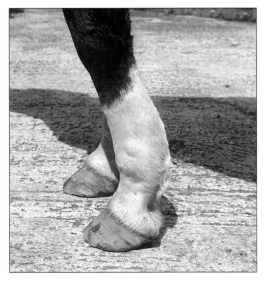

Filled legs Oedematous fluid accumulates in the lower legs (particularly the hind). After initial stiffness, the swelling will reduce quite quickly with gentle exercise. Filled legs are often caused by enforced rest, too little exercise, or vigorous exercise followed by a rest day. Older horses are more disposed to this problem.

Splints A splint is a bony lump where the splint bone joins the cannon bone, a 'spot weld' due to damage to the ligament which attaches the bones together. Occasionally the lump may be due to a fracture of the splint bone. There will be inflammation which develops into a fibrous, then bony lump. The horse will flinch if the area is pressed with the leg held off the ground, although visible swelling may not appear for several days. Splints occasionally appear fully formed almost overnight. Pain and lameness are not usually severe.

Splints can be caused by stress, concussion, injury, poor foot balance and an incorrect calcium/phosphorous ratio to the diet. They are more common in young horses as the ligament tends to fuse with age.

Bursal enlargements These are fluid-filled swellings caused by distension of the tendon sheaths or joint capsules. They rarely cause lameness but are a sign of wear and tear.

The Foot

Bruised sole Most lameness originates in the foot, a common injury being a bruised sole, and may be constant or intermittent and worse on uneven or stony ground. The area is painful when pressed with hoof testers and there will be heat in the foot and a stronger digital pulse.

Puncture Leads to infection and build-up of pus. These wounds usually close up immediately leaving no obvious indication of the point of entry. The symptom is lameness which becomes progressively worse and can be severe. There will be heat in the foot, pain when hoof testers are used, and there may be swelling of the leg together with a strong digital pulse.

Thrush (bacterial infection of the frog) This is caused by standing in wet bedding or wet mud and by insufficient picking out of the feet. Deep-clefted frogs where there is insufficient frog pressure are especially prone. Symptoms: the cleft of the frog softens to exude a black, sticky substance which has a strong, unpleasant smell. In the early stages it does not cause lameness unless the condition is neglected when it will affect the underlying sensitive tissues and cause the horse to go lame.

Laminitis Inflammation of the sensitive laminae of the foot caused by systemic disturbance of the whole body.

It is usually caused by eating too much rich food, especially if the animal is already susceptible to the disease. Ponies at grass in the spring or under-exercised animals in fat condition

Thrush develops in the cleft of the frog. The area should be kept thoroughly clean and anti-bacterial sprays may be used to prevent reinfection.

are most prone, but it is possible for all breeds to develop the disease. Animals whose feet have been allowed to become too long at the toe are more at risk. Cortisone injections may well trigger laminitis, particularly in high-risk animals. Old horses with pituitary cancer (Cushing's syndrome) are also predisposed.

Symptoms Both front feet are usually affected but occasionally all four. The horse stands with the hind-feet tucked under, fore-feet pushed forward in front of it, with the weight on the heels. He may lie down. He will be reluctant to move, will be in pain and may sweat, blow and have a raised temperature and/or pulse. The feet will not necessarily be hot. If forced to move the horse will take short shuffling steps on the heels. In the early stages the symptoms may be minor, e.g. slight soreness and discomfort together with general malaise and possible loss of appetite.

Sprained, torn or bruised muscles Common causes are sudden uncontrolled movements, e.g. slipping or falling or getting cast or a blow or kick. Most common sites are the back and hindquarters – hind-limb lameness; shoulder and neck muscles – fore-limb lameness.

The symptoms are most likely to be lameness which may be relatively short-lived and wear off with gently exercise. There will possibly be heat, swelling, or accumulation of blood or serum under the skin (haematoma).

Muscles usually heal a lot faster than tendons. If there is no obvious heat, pain or swelling, it is difficult to test by manipulation.

Arthritis Arthritic conditions usually develop due to excess stresses on the joints from poor conformation, strain or jarring, or as a sequel to an injury. There may be an hereditary factor involved. Bony growths may develop but often there is nothing obvious to see. Lameness may be

intermittent, worse on hard or uneven ground and may ease as the horse warms up.

Navicular Syndrome This is an increasingly common cause of lameness. There is damage to the navicular bone and associated structures causing pain in the back of the foot. Lameness varies in severity. The causes are not well understood but poor foot shape and balance are involved (*see Chapter Seven*).

Parasitic Worms

These effect all horses but those kept at grass are most at risk.

The life-cycle The eggs pass out in the droppings and hatch into larvae (in only a few days in the right warm, moist conditions). The horse eats the larvae which then migrate via various major organs and blood vessels, before returning to the gut as egg-laying adults.

Redworms (strongyles), large and small The larvae can cause severe damage to the gut, other organs and blood vessels, often resulting in colic.

Ascarids (whiteworms) A particular problem in young horses; adults develop an immunity to them. The larvae cause coughing, bronchitis, pneumonia, 'summer cold', high temperature and runny nose, and liver damage. The adult worms irritate the gut wall, interfering with food absorption, and may cause blockage of the intestines.

Tapeworms These can be up to 80-cm (31-inches) long in segments which can be easily seen when passed in the dung. They can cause damage to the gut wall and impacted colic by blocking the digestive tract.

Seatworms The adult worms live in the caecum and colon. The female lays sticky yellow eggs in and around the anus (these cause irritation) and cause the horse to rub its tail. Other than a rubbed tail the damage is insignificant.

Lungworms These frequently affect donkeys without causing any symptoms. Horses will catch them from grazing used by affected donkeys but rarely from other horses as they do not usually reach the egg-laying stage in the horse.

The larvae get to the lungs but do not fully develop. They cause severe irritation to the linings of the small airways causing coughing, increased mucus and constricted airways.

The symptoms are similar to COPD and even when the cause is removed the horse may continue to be sensitive to dust and fungal spores.

Bot flies The bee-like fly lays sticky yellow eggs on the hairs of the horse's body – particularly the legs and belly – during mid to late summer. Often, the flies frighten horses into galloping around, although they don't sting. The horse licks the eggs and the hatched larvae are swallowed, overwintering in the stomach and feeding on the horse's food. They look like fat maggots. In spring they let go of the stomach wall and pass out in the droppings. They pupate in the ground and the fly emerges in midsummer (one to three months later).

Damage is caused to the stomach wall and in severe cases the stomach may rupture.

Warbles Warbles are becoming rare and their normal host is usually the cow. They are large flies resembling bees which lay sticky eggs at the bases of the horse's hairs. The larvae hatch, burrow into the skin and eventually migrate to the skin of the back area, causing small swellings with air-holes. If undamaged, the maggot should emerge in about a month and fall to the ground to pupate. Hot fomentations or poultices (not kaolin) help ripen

the maggot. After it has popped out, treat as for an open wound. If an abscess forms, call the vet.

Diagnosing a worm problem

All horses carry a worm burden. Lack of regular worming and exposure to heavily contaminated pasture compound the problem. Young horses are particularly at risk as they have not yet developed immunity. Blood tests will indicate infestation.

Your horse may be heavily infested but show no symptoms. However, the following are indications of a problem:
He is a poor doer
He has a big belly while neck and quarters remain poor and ribby
He has a rough staring coat
He has anaemia
He is lacking in energy
He has scouring (diahorrea)
He has colic
He is coughing
He has bronchitis or pneumonia

Treatment Wormers can be given in powder or granule form mixed with the feed, or by oral syringe. Correct care of the pasture is essential. Remember that a dirty stable will also harbour eggs and larvae. Worm horses often to avoid as many worms as possible from developing into egg-laying adults in the gut and eventually contaminating the pasture. Take your vet's advice to avoid the possibility of worms and their offspring becoming resistant to a particular drug. Control the number of migrating larvae.

Adult horses should be wormed every six to ten weeks depending on the drug. In moist summer weather this can be reduced to every four weeks. Never under-dose, check your horse's weight as accurately as possible. Remove bot fly eggs daily.

If introducing a new horse to the pasture or moving horses to clean pasture, keep them stabled for one or two days after worming to ensure all egg-laying adults are dead before you turn them out to grass and that any remaining eggs have been passed out.

All horses living on the same property should be wormed with the same product at the same time to avoid problems of resistance. Take your vet's advice.

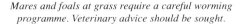

Mares and foals at grass require a careful worming programme. Veterinary advice should be sought.

Nursing care

1. Handle sympathetically, keeping the horse calm, comfortable, quiet and relaxed.
2. Keep the horse in its own stable unless the area is very busy or isolation is required.
3. Make sure the horse has plenty of fresh air, but avoid draughts.
4. Cut the feed to maintenance rations if the horse is stabled and not exercised. Soft hay, small palatable feeds, e.g. bran and a handful of normal feed (well dampened) together with apples, carrots and fresh cut grass will tempt a horse who is off his food and keep his bowels in working order. Do not give more than this, except on your vet's advice.
5. Keep the bed deep and clean. Avoid raising dust when bedding down.
6. Keep the horse warm and if necessary use stable bandages. Use a sweat rug under other rugs or one which absorbs away the moisture if he is likely to break out into a sweat.
7. Groom lightly or if very unwell rub over with a damp cloth. Hand-pull ears for warmth and comfort. Keep eyes and nose wiped clean. Massage legs, particularly if they tend to fill.
8. Keep a written record of temperature and symptoms which should be checked two to three times a day. Write down the vet's instructions and details of any treatment. Check water consumption and feed (do not leave stale feed in a stable). Give fresh water frequently.
9. Keep the stable clean. If isolation procedure is necessary, keep all equipment separate and clean.

Poulticing Use boracic lint for wounds, strains or sprains and bruising. Apply cold to bruises for the first 24–48 hours, otherwise apply hot (check for comfort).

Apply to injury, carefully following instructions on packaging, and cover with plastic; then cover with gamgee tissue. Bandage not too tightly but enough to hold the dressing in place with elastic, crêpe or stable bandages. Kaolin is used for sprains and bruising. First put liquid paraffin on the leg or use gauze to avoid sticking. Apply on lint and cover with gamgee and bandage. Cold therapy is good for initial bruising before applying a hand-hot poultice.

Cold therapy Can be used to reduce swelling and pain and is useful for all inflammation due to injury, strain, or bruising, particularly in the first 24 hours. Cold therapy is not suitable for infected wounds which require a good blood supply.

Hosing Grease the heels first. Be tactful: start at the foot, working your way up the leg. Use a gentle flow at first and hose for up to 20 minutes two to three times daily.

Ice Wet gamgee, frozen or with ice in between the layers, or even a bag of frozen peas can be applied, but do not apply ice directly to the skin. Continue treatment for approximately 15 minutes and never for longer than 30 minutes.

Cold bandages These combine pressure and cold and there are various types. They can be kept in the deep freeze and taken to competitions in an insulated bag.

Tubbing For cleaning puncture wounds in the foot and relieving bruising. Immerse clean hoof in hand-hot water in a bucket. Add salt or Epsom salts (a handful) which may increase the drawing power. Top up with hot water (very carefully) as necessary. Continue for 10 minutes two to three times a day.

Isolation Procedure

Isolate the infected horse in a stable away from others. Disinfect your feet and hands on leaving the stable and use rubber gloves and overalls. Burn all soiled bedding and keep all equipment separate. Persons responsible for nursing should limit their attention to the sick horse and should thoroughly scrub and disinfect the stable when evidence of the illness has passed. Other horses in the yard may be incubating the disease: check extra carefully for signs of ill-health and avoid causing stress. Hacking-out or competing should not take place while there are infectious diseases in the yard.

Dentistry

Horses' teeth should be checked at least twice a year by a vet or qualified horse dentist. Although most horses will accept it, some find teeth-rasping a traumatic experience and it may be difficult to regain their confidence once frightened. This can have further repercussions, making it more difficult to administer wormers or other drugs by mouth. You should ensure that the horse is well-mannered and will allow his head to be handled easily. Patience and tact on the practitioner's part is then generally all that is necessary. Tell your vet in advance if the horse is head-shy, or has had a bad experience, as it may well be better to sedate him in the first place rather than risk a battle which will only alarm him further.

Opposite
A fit and healthy horse will respond to his owner and a great partnership is sure to develop. This Saddlebred is gleaming with health.

Below
Teeth should be examined twice a year or more if there is a known problem. Rasping is carried out to reduce the sharp edges which form on the teeth.

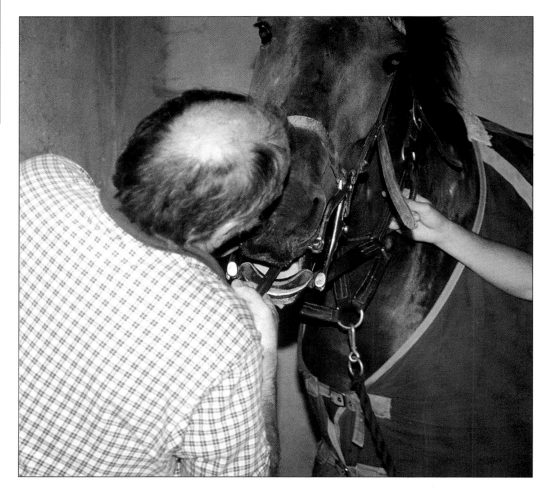

How to take a horse's temperature and pulse

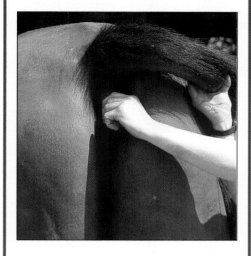

Taking the temperature

First shake down the thermometer and apply petroleum jelly to it. Standing to the side, insert the thermometer and press it gently to the side wall of the rectum. Hold it in place for the prescribed amount of time (check instructions). The horse's normal temperature is 37.5–38°C (99.5–100.4°F). A rise of a degree or more should be taken seriously.

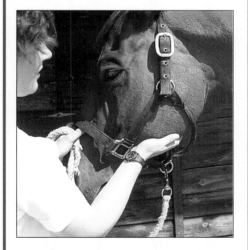

Taking the pulse

A horse's pulse can be taken at various sites, behind the pastern and to either side of the fetlock (the digital pulse) or you can use a stethoscope behind the elbow. The easiest place to feel the pulse is where the artery crosses the inside edge of the jaw-bone, as shown here. Only lightly use your fingers, your thumb has a strong pulse of its own.

Normal pulse at rest is 36–40 beats per minute. Increased pulse and respiration when at rest may be caused by excitement, stress, pain or illness.

Chapter Four
FEEDING YOUR HORSE

Of all the areas connected with horse care, feeding seems to cause the most confusion. This is hardly surprising for an increase in research into the nutrition of horses has changed some of our traditional ideas and added a little more science to the 'art' of feeding. There are many companies now producing whole ranges of compound feeds (cubes and mixes) which are increasingly used instead of traditional grains and there is a bewildering choice of supplements and additives for all occasions.

Rules of Feeding

Feed little and often
All short feed should be well mixed and may be slightly dampened. Give grain or cubes, allowing at least 3 hours between full feeds.
- Feed plenty of bulk (even for horses in very fast work) to maintain good digestion.
- Always go for good quality – inferior feed is uneconomical and may cause digestive and respiratory problems due to dust and moulds. *Storage is important: feed must be kept absolutely dry and inaccessible to vermin.*
- Feed at regular times – this avoids stress and possible loss of condition/colic.
- Feed from clean receptacles.
- Make any changes to feedstuffs gradually over several days, *but reduce short feed dramatically in cases of enforced rest.*
- Clean, fresh water must be available at all times. *Do not let the horse drink large quantities immediately after a feed or when it is still hot and blowing.*
- Feed according to work-load, age and condition.
- Feed according to the weight and type of horse.
- Feed something succulent every day. This is appetizing, adds variety and is a source of added fibre and minerals.
- Allow at least 1 hour after the horse has finished feeding before exercising.

Water

Water is vital for life and health. Without it a horse will survive only a short time. 50–70% of the horse's bodyweight is water and a loss of between 8 and 15% can cause dehydration and illness.

One horse will consume approximately 45 litres (10 gallons) a day, depending on weather conditions, how hard it is working (and therefore sweating) and the moisture content of its food. For

example, a horse eating a great deal of dry hay will need to drink more water to help the digestive process: too little may lead to colic.

In hot weather, frequent access to water is essential before, during, and after exercise to prevent dehydration. Even in the final hour before fast work small amounts can be allowed. During the cooling-down process after fast work, wait until the horse has stopped blowing then offer small quantities (approx. 2.2 litres/4 pints) which should be offered every 10–15 minutes until the horse is no longer thirsty.

Horses should be provided with fresh water at all times when stabled and in the field. In circumstances such as these, few will drink enough in one go, even straight after a feed or before or after work, to cause a digestive disturbance or colic. Horses are particularly fussy in this respect. They have their own preferences: some insist on water being very fresh, practically drinking it from the tap, while others prefer the taste of the field supply and will have a long drink when they are turned out. All object to stale, dusty, water tainted with ammonia from bedding or with particles of food or bedding floating in it. The horse which leaves an inch or two of water in the bottom of his bucket is more likely to be fastidious rather than not thirsty. Some will go thirsty rather than drink from an unfamiliar bucket or one with a new smell. Unusual flavours such as water from a container or from a different part of the country may be viewed with great suspicion, causing problems when travelling. Try to get horses accustomed to different tastes before you travel or

try adding peppermint to the water at home and then using it to disguise the different taste of the water while you are away.

Grass

The horse's natural food, grass is a wonderful conditioner, but can vary hugely in quality and one horse's paradise may be another's poison.

Beautifully kept paddocks with large proportions of the most nutritious grasses are ideal for Thoroughbreds, but could be literally fatal to a native pony with a metabolism designed to utilize the roughest grazing. Old, established pasture, with a variety of grasses and herbs, well tended but not over-fertilized, is the ideal option. Spring and early summer grass has the highest food value with a possibility of an autumn flush in warm, damp weather. Food value declines considerably during the winter months although, in sufficient quantity, the grass will still provide valuable roughage. Alone, it is insufficient to keep all but the hardiest ponies satisfied.

The hay/grass side of the diet is very important. Remember to take into account the amount and quality of the grass the horse is eating as in spring and summer he may need little else.

Hay

The best hay is made from grass cut in late spring to midsummer when there is plenty of leaf and before the seeds have dropped and the stalks have coarsened. Good-quality hay which has been well made will be sweet-smelling and free from dust and mould. Hay baled while damp will deteriorate and go quickly mouldy. Hay which has been baled too tightly tends to be dusty.

When a bale is opened it should spring apart and the slabs or sections should be easy to loosen and shake up.

Hay which has lain out in the fields for too long (usually due to the weather) will appear washed out and bleached, as will hay cut late in a hot summer. Coarse, stalky hay (cut late) will be of inferior food value and horses do not generally like it. Hay containing weeds, reeds, etc., should be avoided. It will probably be of poor quality and some weeds, such as ragwort, may be poisonous.

The food value of hay varies enormously

Above
A carefully planned diet is essential for all horses. The owner should give best quality feed and should ensure a balanced diet relevant to the horse's breed, size, temperament and work-load.

Opposite
Large rubber feed bowls are safe and unbreakable. Use scoups to measure correct amounts.

depending on the type of grasses used, the quality of the soil and type of fertilizers added, when it was cut, how quickly and carefully it was made and how it has been stored.

Poor-quality hay, particularly if dusty or, worse still, mouldy, will cause digestive and respiratory problems *(see page 29)*. It is false economy to feed inferior hay and the food value of your hay will make more difference to your horse's condition than just about anything else. It is best to wait until early autumn before feeding hay made that year as new hay tends to be indigestible. If you have no choice but to feed it, introduce it very gradually. The same applies when introducing hay from a different source, even if it appears to be the same type as previously used.

Hay must be kept dry. Raise bales above the ground on pallets or a layer of straw bales. Leave an air gap between bales and the sides of walls. Do not site a barn in a damp enclosed area; hay keeps better if stored initially in a Dutch barn. Newly-made hay kept in a small enclosed shed will tend to become dusty. There are two main types of hay:

Meadow hay

Hay cut from permanent pasture. This varies greatly in food value depending on the type of grasses and how the fields are managed. Beware of weeds. It should be greenish in colour, long and leafy and smell sweet. It is suitable for ponies and, depending on quality, for horses in light to medium work and mares and foals.

Seed hay

Hay cut from grasses and other plants grown as an annual crop. It is usually more nutritious and has higher protein content than meadow hay, and includes selected grasses such as rye-grass and timothy as well as clover. It will be coarser and harder than meadow hay. Ideally cut in late spring, it is suitable for horses in medium–hard work.

The quality is more important than the type of hay. Good meadow hay is preferable to poorly made seed hay and horses do not appreciate very soft or very coarse hay. However, horses and ponies in light work which are considered to be 'good doers' may well appreciate larger quantities of hay which is of lower food-value to very restricted amounts of high quality.

Soaking hay is essential before feeding it to horses with an allergy to fungal spores and dust. Always use fresh water and a large, clean container. Opinions vary as to how long the hay should be left to soak, from 10 minutes to overnight, but the consensus of opinion is that it should be soaked until all the hay is thoroughly wet. The aim is to swell the fungal spores so that they adhere to the stems and cannot be inhaled. If left too long the soluble carbohydrates will leach out and fermentation may occur, especially in hot weather. Feeding icy hay may cause colic. Hay can also be steamed but this is less effective than soaking.

Haylage

This is grass that is cut earlier than it is for hay so that it retains higher protein levels and is more nutritious. The grass is left to partially dry, then vacuum-packed in plastic-covered bales where fermentation occurs. It remains dust-free and has high energy levels. It is good for horses with breathing problems but is expensive and each bale must be used up within a few days of opening as it does not keep well, especially in hot weather. It is produced in varying types but even the least nutritious will compare very favourably with hay so it must be fed with care and concentrate levels reduced. Feed according to the manufacturer's instructions.

Haynets with extra-small holes help extend the eating time and reduce boredom. Feeding extra fibre such as chaff, sugar-beet and root vegetables will help assuage hunger.

Farmers are now commonly producing 'big bale' haylage as well as hay. It must be well made, weed-free and not taken from field margins where dirt and debris may adhere causing abnormal fermentation. When ready to use, let the bale stand unwrapped and check it thoroughly.

Any bags, even if slightly punctured, should be discarded; this applies to all types of haylage. *Do not suddenly change from one type of fibre to another, e.g. hay to haylage. This can cause colic.*

Do not feed if there is mould present. This may cause respiratory or digestive problems; discoloured or black mould may be very poisonous.

Opened bales used for horses with COPD should not be kept with hay or straw.

Other hay substitutes

If you cannot obtain hay of an acceptable quality there are various other feeds which will supply the horse with sufficient fibre. Oat straw is low in protein and energy and it will need to be supplemented with concentrate feed other than perhaps for native ponies. There is a small risk of impacted colic if too much is fed. Oat chaff, alfalfa or grass chaff are suitable for animals suffering from laminitis. Other alternatives are high-fibre complete cubes and sugar-beet.

Chaff This is chopped hay or straw and the bought variety can sometimes be of poor quality, though there are many reputable manufacturers who produce quality oat straw, alfalfa and dried grass chaffs. Many large yards have their own chaff cutter. The chaffs must not smell musty or be dusty. They are often mixed with molasses to make them more appetizing but can, nevertheless, still deteriorate fairly quickly. Chaff helps improve digestion, encouraging horses to eat more slowly and chew more thoroughly. Add 1–3 double handfuls to the feed.

Alfalfa – chaff or cubes This is highly nutritious, having high levels of protein and is also high in calcium and other minerals: it can be fed to resting or convalescing horses.

Sugar-beet Sold as cubes, which are easier to store, or as dried beet pulp, it is usually mixed with molasses. It is high in calcium and when mixed with traditional grains helps to correct the calcium/phosphorus ratio. It is appetizing and a good source of slow-release, non-heating energy for horses in light–moderate work and is usually fed in winter, though it is too bulky to be fed to horses in hard work. Generally feed 450–900 g (1–2 lb) dry weight per day but more is sometimes fed (particularly as a partial substitute for hay).
Preparation Sugar-beet must be soaked or it will swell in the stomach and cause severe colic.
Beet pulp – soak 2:1 per volume water/beet, 12–24 hours.
Cubes – 4:1 per volume water/beet, 24 hours. Prepare daily: be extra careful in warm weather as fermentation may occur when it should not then be fed to horses. There is a prepared sugar-beet now on the market which does not need soaking but which is more expensive. Seek your vet's advice before using it.

Oats This is considered the ideal grain for feeding to horses. Whole oats should be plump, hard, and shiny and can be fed to horses in hard work. Bruising or crushing makes them more digestible. The kernel, however, should not be damaged and they should smell sweet. Avoid oats that are dusty or appear to be all husks. Feed within 3 weeks of bruising as food value and vitamins decrease after this. They are suitable for horses in medium–hard work. Oats have a heating effect so are not usually suitable for ponies.

Barley The whole grains appear shorter and more diamond-shaped than oats and they have very hard husks. They are fed rolled, micronized (cooked in a microwave oven), flaked (heat-treated) or boiled, never whole, when they are indigestible.
Barley is usually less heating than oats and a little more fattening. It is also lower in fibre: therefore feed up to 50% of the concentrate ration only, usually only 450–700 g (1–1½ lb a day), if boiled. Take care as some horses are allergic to barley and come out in bumps or a rash under the skin.
Preparation For boiled barley, simmer with plenty of water for 2–3 hours until the grains have

Oats

Mixed flakes of yellow maize and barley with peas

Good quality bran is hard to come by. This sample is not too 'floury'

swollen and burst and are soft and slightly sticky.

Maize This is fed flaked or micronized. It has the appearance of thick cornflakes and should be sweet-smelling and dust-free. It is high-energy with less fibre, so mix with chaff or other grains. Useful for fattening and warmth it is, however, very heating. Feed a maximum of 900–1350 g (2–3 lb) or 25% ration per day. Mostly fed as part of a 'mix'.

Bran The inner husk of the wheat grain, it should have broad, pinkish, sweet-smelling, floury flakes. It is low in energy and its main value is its laxative property when fed damp. Its softness makes it palatable to old or ill horse. Small amounts (about 450 g (1 lb) can be fed daily or as a mash. The use of a bran mash after hard work is now generally not advised as it is indigestible and any sudden change to the diet should be avoided. Calcium-phosphorus ratio is 1:7 (very poor) and if bran is fed in other than the smallest quantities a limestone flour supplement should be added.
Preparation To make a bran mash, put 900–1350 g (2–3 lb) bran in a bucket. Pour boiling water over and stir. The result should be wet but not sloppy. Add some salt and possibly a handful of oats for taste. Place a sack over the bucket and let is 'cook' until cool enough to eat. (Check by plunging your hand into the bran to check that it is not still very hot in the middle.) Add carrots, apples, supplements, etc. just before feeding.
Note: Boiled feeds, mashes and sugar-beet should be fed immediately as they will quickly sour.

Cubes There are many different brands and varieties of cubes or pellets. Choose well known brands with good quality control. They should be dry, quite hard and have an appetizing smell. A damp, crumbly or stale-smelling product must not be fed.
They are composed of a mixture of different grains, peas and beans, grass and additives, compressed into pellets.

Coarse mix 'Muesli' for horses, this is a loose mixture of grains and similar constituents to those found in cubes. Fibre content varies according to type – usually high for non-heating meadow mix types, low for competition mixes. They are usually combined with molasses or glucose syrup, making them palatable and dust-free. High fibre with high energy and low sugar varieties are now available.
Cubes and mixes are formulated in entire ranges with different types to suit every kind of horse and level of activity. They have a distinct advantage in that they are nutritionally balanced and of consistent quality as well as easy to feed and store. They are more expensive than traditional grains. There is plenty of advertising literature specifying the exact contents and suitability of each make and type.

Micronized feeds These, e.g. barley, are cooked in a microwave oven to improve digestibility and therefore available energy and fattening properties.

Horse cubes are high in fibre and low in sugar

Extruded feeds These look rather like popcorn and are designed to be easily digested, allowing them to be fed in smaller quantities. They are good for putting on condition though not very appetizing. Always check the 'sell by' date for freshness and the vitamin/mineral content.

Linseed This is the seed of the flax plant. It is fattening, with high levels (though poor in quality) of protein. Because of its high oil content it is good for the coat. Feed 225 g (8 oz) dry weight 2–3 times a week. Good in a mash.
Preparation Linseed is poisonous if poorly prepared. Soak overnight in cold water, then bring to the boil. Boil hard for at least 10 minutes, then simmer until the seeds are soft. Can be fed as linseed tea or jelly, depending on the amount of liquid with which it has been mixed.

Supplements and Additives

Vitamins and minerals in the right quantities and balance are essential to the horse's health. Good quality cubes and coarse mixes are correctly balanced while hay and cereals may have deficiencies. Check the total feed makes adequate provision. There are many broad-spectrum vitamin and mineral supplements available, as well as formulations to combat particular deficiencies and for young horses, high performance animals, etc. Salt is vital, especially when the horse sweats profusely after exertion. Provide a salt lick or at least 25g (1oz) a day to the feed. A calcium/phosphorus ratio of between 1 and 2:1 for adults and up to 4:1 for youngsters is necessary for good bone growth. Feeding carrots and cod liver oil will provide extra vitamins A and D in the winter months.

Herbal supplements are very popular for a whole range of ailments and problems of temperament.

Feed 'balancers' are mixes or pellets containing high levels of vitamins, minerals and essential amino acids to redress any deficiencies in a traditional cereal/hay diet and provide essential nutrients. They are fed in small quantities and can also be given to 'good doers' who require very little short feed.

Feed additives which promote good digestion such as certain clays and pro-biotics (live cultures of 'friendly' bacteria which improve the function of the large intestine) may also improve the temperament by reducing the affects of poor digestion which produce agitation in 'hot' horses.

Whatever you decide to try, check that the product has been properly researched and is formulated specifically for horses.

For horses in very hard and demanding work, supplements become even more important. This is a complicated subject which you should discuss with your vet. The right balance is needed for maximum performance but feeding too much, or mixing supplements, can cause problems.

Special Diets and Considerations

Very cold weather Only a little more feed is needed and none at all if the horse is stabled and

Sugar-beet cubes. They must be soaked for 24 hours before feeding

Chaff and molasses

Coarse mix

well protected with rugs. Over-kindness and reduced exercise could result in azoturia/laminitis or a very agitated animal.

Very cold water can deter a horse from drinking, resulting in impacted colic. Add hot water to frozen buckets or troughs, if practicable.

An abundance of good hay is important to a horse living out, especially when there is frost and snow: give high-fibre concentrate feeds as necessary; boiled feeds are fattening and warming. Haylage is easier to use than soaked hay in very cold weather, but do not change to it suddenly or colic may result.

Old horses If your horse is getting on in years but still looking and going well on normal feeding,

this is fine. If not, check his general health, soundness, whether or not he needs worming, and his general comfort. His teeth may need to be rasped every few months and they may be worn to such an extent that hay or grass cannot be properly chewed. He will require higher levels of minerals, vitamins and good quality protein. An ideal feed is veteran mix, specially designed for elderly horses. You can also feed him soft food for worn teeth such as boiled feed, bran, sugar-beet, alfalfa, chaff and soft meadow hay; you can even soak his cubes to soften them. Overall, he may need more food to maintain condition but avoid over-feeding and follow your vet's advice.

Young horses Higher amounts of protein are needed until youngsters are 2–3 years old. They also require higher levels of vitamins and minerals, the quality and balance being important, and it is essential that they have sufficient calcium and phosphorus in the correct ratio. It is important to avoid over-feeding as young horses which become too fat can suffer from joint and growth problems. Feed good quality hay and stud cubes or mix. Good grazing is also an important factor in the growth and well-being of the young horse.

Convalescence After illness, a special diet may be needed to build up the horse's strength. There are special convalescence diets on the market which are suitable for recuperating horses.

An enforced rest may cause loss of muscle over the neck, back and quarters. Be careful not to over-feed in an attempt to improve this problem. As long as the horse's overall condition is good, the lost muscle development and 'top line' will return with the correct balance of feed and work.

Thin Horses Some are naturally lean but stress and a hyperactive personality can prevent weight gain as can underlying illness. Divide non-heating fattening concentrates into smaller feeds or give more at night. Good grass and hay can work wonders.

Fat Horses Reduce total amounts of feed and restrict quality and quantity of hay and grass. Increase amount but not speed of exercise if the horse is obese. Moderate amounts of oats may liven up a lazy horse, assisting weight loss.

Suiting the Rider

Horses can dramatically change personality depending on what and how much they are fed.
To calm Feed a low-energy, high-fibre diet, such as hay, horse and pony cubes, pasture mix, sugar-beet without added molasses. Avoid oats, too much barley, high-sugar compound feeds and those designed for medium to heavy work.
For extra zip Feed oats, high-energy compound feeds such as competition mix, good quality hay. Avoid giving excessive amounts of fibre.

Working out what to feed your horse, and how much, may seem complicated at first, but if you follow the simple stages set out below you will find planning a diet quite straightforward.

The tricky part, which can only be learned

from experience, observation, and the application of plenty of common sense, is assessing if your horse's diet is exactly right for him. The aim should be a contented, enthusiastic horse, gleaming with health and in the right mental and physical condition to perform his job. It is equally important to gain as much technical knowledge of the subject as possible until you can trust your own instinct as to what adjustments to make.

Some horses will respond quite dramatically to small changes of diet, becoming either very quiet or agitated, or even colicky. Others will gradually lose or gain weight and may appear lacklustre, slightly more tense or more easily frightened. A dull, staring coat, lacking in lustre, may indicate vitamin and mineral deficiencies and this may later manifest itself in the condition of the hooves *(see Chapter Seven)*

When problems arise, act the detective, and check out every aspect of the horse's care to discover where the imbalance has occurred.

It is important to remember to adjust the feed to meet a change in circumstances, especially a sudden reduction in the amount of exercise (maybe you get flu or the horse loses a shoe). You should reduce the feed the night before and the day on which you cannot exercise the horse. If possible, turn him out to graze or at least lead him out by hand. If he must have box rest for any reason, cut out concentrates altogether, other than a handful plus chaff and succulents.

Horses are very much individuals. If your

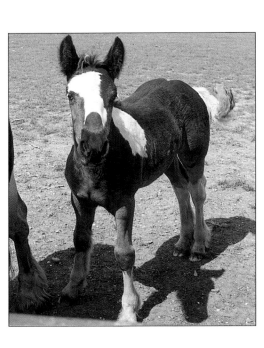

Above
Young horses and foals will need a carefully planned diet to ensure healthy, strong bones.

Opposite
Energy and vitality can only be accomplished by correct feeding.

horse looks and performs well, and appears to be happy on his present diet, don't be tempted to adjust it just because he is getting more or less than the experts say he should or because the feed companies have developed yet another range of wonder feed!

Feeding Example
A 16.1hh middleweight all-rounder in medium work, stabled in winter.

Weight	500 kg (1100 lb)
Total feed	12.5 kg (27^1/2 lb)
Good quality (65%) **meadow or seed hay**	8.2 kg (18 lb)
Total concentrates (consisting of)	(35%) 4.3 kg (9^1/2 lb) **Oats** 2.7 kg (6 lb) **Barley** 900 g (2 lb) or **Medium-energy mix** 3.6 kg (8 lb) **Alfalfa chaff** 450 g (1 lb) **Sugar-beet** 225 g (^{1}/2 lb) **Carrots**

This could be adjusted to increase the short feed/decrease the bulk a little, depending on the horse's condition and behaviour.

What to Feed and How Much

There is a formula which is really quite simple. *Remember it is only a guide.*
- First establish your horse's weight (one way is to use a weigh tape.
- Every day, the average horse will need to eat an amount equal to 2^1/2% of his body weight.
- The chart below gives approximate weights with the required amounts of food for each.

Table of approximate weights:

Type & height	Approx Weight		Total Feed	
	kg	lb	kg	lb
13.2hh pony	255	560	6.3	14
14.2hh cob	400	880	10	22
15.2hh small hunter type	450	990	11.25	25
16.3hh Thoroughbred	500	1100	12.5	27^1/2
16.3 heavy hunter type	600	1320	15	33

(1 kg = 2.2 lb)

Next think about the type of work the horse will be doing. As a rule, the harder and faster he works, the more concentrate he will require. This chart shows how to split the diet into bulk (hay and grass) and concentrates (short feed).

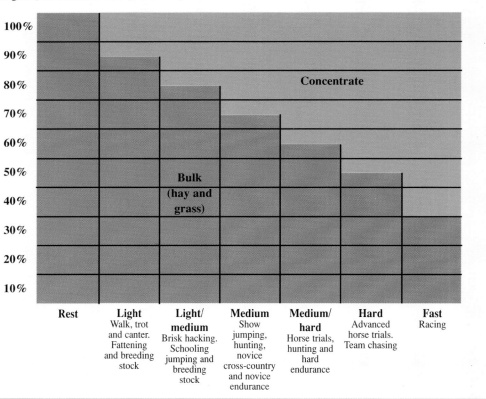

Concentrate

Bulk (hay and grass)

| 100% | 90% | 80% | 70% | 60% | 50% | 40% | 30% | 20% | 10% |

| Rest | Light Walk, trot and canter. Fattening and breeding stock | Light/ medium Brisk hacking. Schooling jumping and breeding stock | Medium Show jumping, hunting, novice cross-country and novice endurance | Medium/ hard Horse trials, hunting and hard endurance | Hard Advanced horse trials. Team chasing | Fast Racing |

Chapter Five
GETTING HORSES FIT

Everyone knows that event horses and racehorses need to be brought to a peak of fitness; but what about the horses and ponies doing all manner of other tasks? How many have been consciously trained for the job they do, to the relevant level of fitness for the type of work in hand. For example, an endurance horse with the stamina to keep going for many miles would not do well in a sprint race requiring short bursts of speed.

How fit does your horse need to be for his present life-style? Think of the most strenuous work he is called upon to do. Does he cope well?

Blowing heavily, excessive sweating and slow recovery after exertion are obvious signs that the horse is not fit enough; there are more subtle signs. Paces becoming flat or less rhythmical, as well as stumbling or tripping, may be signs of fatigue but could equally be caused by boredom, laziness and lack of attention. A really enthusiastic animal may literally go until he drops. It is up to you to gauge how much he can physically withstand and resist the temptation to do too much. You may know a horse which starts a cross-country course jumping boldly and well, only to lean more and more on the rider's hands (not necessarily slowing down) and towards the end of

the course is misjudging his stride, hitting fences and maybe refusing or eventually crashing through one. This is very likely caused by fatigue – possibly exacerbated by an unfit rider unable to keep the horse balanced between leg and hand.

Whatever your eventual goal, the initial fitness programme will be much the same. Some people may be taking short cuts and appearing to get away with them but the horse's general health and soundness will suffer in the long term. The early slow and steady work is crucial. The more jumping and fast work you intend to do the more important it is to do a thorough job of hardening and strengthening the horse's limbs before he undergoes any form of added stress.

There is no need to do exactly the same amount of work every day or even necessarily to ride every day. In fact, every horse needs easier days to recover from hard work. A horse cannot stay at peak fitness indefinitely. It comes down again to common sense. If, for example, you like to go to shows, hunt or go on long hacks at the weekend, your horse needs enough exercise in the week to keep up his levels of fitness without over-stressing or tiring him. It is all a question of balance. It is asking for trouble to work the horse hardly at all during the week and then take him for

a gallop on Saturday just because he feels too lively. The more intense the exertion, the greater the need for a holiday, for a time for rest and repair. This is one of the reasons why eventers, hunters and top-level show-jumpers have seasons, with periods of complete rest or very light work in between. A general riding horse, under less stress, can stay in work all year, having a couple of weeks off when his owner goes on holiday together with easy spells due more to his owner's other commitments, or the state of the weather, than to any positive planning. A change of scene is often as important as a rest to freshen the horse's outlook. Hunting has given many a jaded show horse a new lease of life; varied hacking and some jumping are more fun than existing on a solid diet of dressage schooling.

It is quite possible to get a horse too fit: some horses thrive on exercise, getting stronger and livelier the more they get. The rider works the horse harder to settle him and only succeeds in getting him fitter. This is where some lateral thinking is required: perhaps a longer spell in the field each day, lower-energy short feed (or less of it), longer but slower work, or a calming but varied schedule will make all the difference.

Bringing up from grass
Check that the horse is sound and in good health. It is a good idea to give him his flu/anti-tetanus booster a week or two before he starts work, though some prefer to administer it before his rest period in case he reacts adversely to it. Have his teeth checked and rasped, if necessary, and get him shod. Keep to his regular worming programme unless you are bringing him in completely or changing fields; if so, this is the time to worm him. Check his tack at the same time and that it still fits.

The change in diet should be gradual. It is a good idea to accustom him to eating some concentrates while he is still living at grass; otherwise, start with very small feeds (or bran mashes if the droppings are too firm). Feed meadow hay and increase the concentrates while decreasing the hay as the work builds up.

When starting exercise, if you wish, you can begin working the horse lightly from the field for the first week or two. In fact some people keep their horses 'ticking over' with light work throughout their rest period which helps maintain muscle tone.

If you are working the horse after a long rest period, harden off his back with methylated spirits/salt water or surgical spirit for a week before commencing. Use a soft girth and numnah and check for any swellings or sore places, which are less likely if you build the level of work gradually. It is a good idea to divide his exercise into two sessions.

Get him used to being stabled by bringing him in with a companion for a couple of hours a day and gradually building up until he is in all night or day depending on the weather. If you have to bring him in suddenly, immediately feed bran mashes, succulents and hay for the first couple of days – this is least advisable if it can be avoided.

Some problems may arise once the horse is stabled. He may develop digestive problems due to a sudden increase in dry fibre; this could result in an impacted colic, so change his diet over as gradually as possible. He may start coughing due to dust – take precautions (*see COPD, page 29*). He may develop temperamental problems due to confinement, such as weaving, crib-biting and box-walking. These can be alleviated by turning him daily out to grass, even when fit. An hour a day with a quiet companion in a not too lush field will help him relax and bring mental and physical improvements. Overall, try to create a calm enjoyable environment.

A traditional exercise programme
To produce a horse fit enough for one-day events will take approximately 12 weeks. The programme divides up into three more or less equal sections of work – slow/development/fast. The work you do in

the third section will depend on the horse's job and can incorporate lower-key versions of the final task.

Start with at least two weeks' walking, building up from a half to one and a half hours duration and keeping to smooth, even going or quiet roads.

If the horse is very excitable you may have to work him in a confined space or lunge him first – but build up gradually to avoid stress on unfit limbs and muscles. Only lunge as much as is necessary to take the edge off his exuberance.

By the third week, begin short steady trots in straight lines and gradually build up the trot work to about one-third of total. From week four you can start schooling on the flat and lungeing, starting gently with large circles and easy movements.

In week six, initiate steady, short canters. You can then gradually increase their duration until, by week ten, he can canter steadily for about 10 minutes without distress.

As the programme develops, gradually introduce varied work. Ride him over countryside, hills and uneven terrain. Take in small jumps and natural obstacles such as water and ditches.

Many people, however, use **interval training** *(see Glossary)*. Every fourth day, after a thorough warm up, the horse is cantered steadily for two or three spells with short rests in walk in between to allow partial recovery. Pulse and respiration rates help the rider to gauge the amount of exertion and the recovery rate and so monitor the development of fitness with reduced risk of strain.

Towards the end of the programme you can take part in small competitions, keeping to steady speeds at first.

If you are interested in hunter-trialing or eventing or in long-distance riding, make sure you gradually include work similar to that which will eventually be required. Long hacks with the occasional short fast one will suit the long-distance horse but the horse required to gallop must practise a certain amount of fast work. If there is nowhere suitable to gallop, slower work uphill will help and exerts less strain on the horse's tendons. Increasingly longer periods of brisk cantering are better than too much galloping, particularly if the ground is hard or holding.

Check for coughing or laboured breathing, heat or swelling in tendons or joints (even if the horse is sound), muscular stiffness, saddle/girth galls or any tenderness in the back region. Dealing with slight problems at an early stage will save time and more serious conditions from developing.

During the programme, be aware of your horse's response to the work and stop if he appears distressed. Increase the work-load only when he appears to be coping well, not breathing too heavily and recovering quickly, eager to continue after a period of trot or canter.

Remember that an excitable horse and one that is eager to please will carry on regardless: a lazy one may need prompting and can be encouraged by working alongside a more energetic companion.

Care after work

We are considering here a horse that has just galloped round a cross-country course. The main principles will apply whatever strenuous work the horse has been doing.

However excited or exhausted you are, the horse's care and welfare must be your first concern and doing a good job now will help prevent any ill effects from his exertion.

Slow down gradually. Return the horse to his horse-box, keeping him walking until he has stopped blowing. This will facilitate the flushing out of waste products from the muscles, reducing stiffness the following day. Then remove saddle and boots, quickly checking for injuries.

In cold weather, immediately cover the horse with a rug (the thicker sort of sweat-through rug is ideal). Sponge sweat from head, neck, back and between the legs with warm water.

In hot weather, wash all over (including the hindquarters) with cold water. Reapply cold water frequently for maximum cooling. (Recent research suggests that this will not produce muscle cramps or 'tying up' as previously thought.) Keep walking between washings and once cool, carry on walking him until he is dry.

Once he has stopped blowing, offer water. Give a quarter of a bucket every 10 minutes until he is no longer thirsty; don't let him drink too much at once.

Electrolytes added to water or feed are valuable after fast work to replace essential salts and minerals. Get the horse used to drinking them at home so that when offered a choice between these or plain water he will drink whichever he needs. If he is always reluctant to take them they can be added to his feed or given in an oral paste.

It is now important to trot the horse up to check for soundness. Make a thorough check and treat injuries, including the mouth and back. Check the legs – if there is any sign of swelling, apply ice or other cold therapy *(see page 34)* and contact the vet for advice. Remove studs and check shoes.

After about an hour, give some hay and when fully recovered, take him home as soon as possible. Do not leave him standing outside or in a hot or cold vehicle.

Once home, check again for injuries or swellings. If sweated up, sponge him off and walk him until he is cool before letting him relax with some hay, or, if it is his usual routine, turn him out once he is dry.

If possible, keep to normal feed times but give a small proportion of his normal feed. Groom him enough, but don't fuss. Keep an eye on him for the rest of the day for signs of colic.

Next day

Make sure that he is eating well but keep quantities small – refusing short- feed is a sign of over-excitement, tiredness or impending illness. Check that he is well in himself as hard work can trigger viruses into action. Make sure that he is still sound and that no fresh injuries have appeared.

If all is well, turn out for an hour or so or walk him in hand. Do easy relaxing work for the next few days.

Letting down

This means reducing the horse's level of fitness and acclimatizing him to living out before a period

of rest. It takes a lot less time than getting him fit but you need to take into account the time of year and weather conditions and remember that it will mean a big change for the horse both mentally and physically. Taking 2–3 weeks, gradually reduce exercise and cease thorough grooming to encourage grease build-up in the coat for extra warmth and waterproofing. Reduce short feed and increase bulk. Use fewer rugs, taking the weather into account, and increase turn-out time, always with a companion. If you do not intend to ride the horse at all, remove either all his shoes or just the hind ones.

Chapter Six
CLIPPING

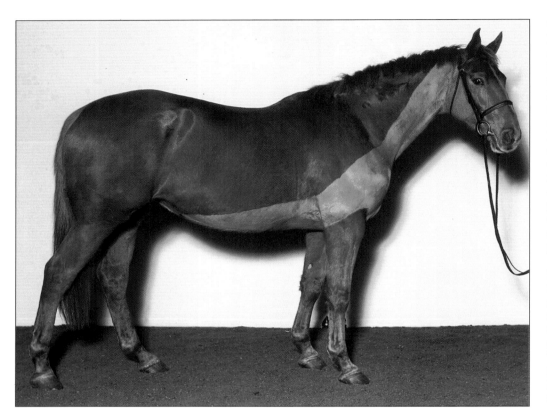

When a horse with a thick winter coat is worked hard he will get hot and distressed and sweat profusely. He will also tend to lose condition and be difficult to dry and groom. A clipped horse will perform better and because he is easier to dry will be less likely to chill, as long as he is not left standing without rugs.

Clipping improves the horse's appearance and makes it easier to keep the skin clean and prevent or control skin diseases such as ringworm, or external parasites such as lice.

It is important to choose the right clip for the type of work the horse is doing and to supply sufficient rugs. A horse with a full or hunter clip may well need an underblanket if turned out in a New Zealand rug, even for an hour or so, and will require an exercise rug when working slowly such as hacking mostly in walk and steady trot.

A cold horse will be unhappy, his muscles will stiffen and he will lose condition. He will also tend to be very fresh when first exercised!

When to clip
When the coat is 'set', usually at the beginning of autumn, then as often as necessary, probably at least twice more, but possibly every 3–4 weeks until the end of winter. Avoid clipping after this as you may affect the summer coat. However, horses which grow heavy coats may need to be clipped later in the year. Some old horses which grow long coats all year, and sometimes eventers or driving horses working in hot weather, will need to be clipped during the summer.

Preparation Clippers should be sufficiently sturdy to cope with the number of horses about to be clipped. They should by well serviced, yearly, if in heavy use. Always check the cable for any signs of damage and that the plug is correctly wired and earthed. Use a power point in a safe position away from the horse: a good place is in the centre of the stable high up on a beam. Make sure that the power point is fitted with a circuit-breaker and check that it is working. It should be positioned as near as possible to the power source, e.g. at the plug.

You will require two pairs of sharpened blades and you can buy coarser blades for clipping the legs. You will also need oil or special clipper spray for the blades and oil for lubricating the motor, if specified. A small brush for removing hair from the blades and air inlets is important and some surgical spirit to clean and cool the blades. The box where clipping is to take place should be large and well lit – fluorescent strip lighting is best. A tie ring with string attached should be used to tether the horse and a haynet to keep him

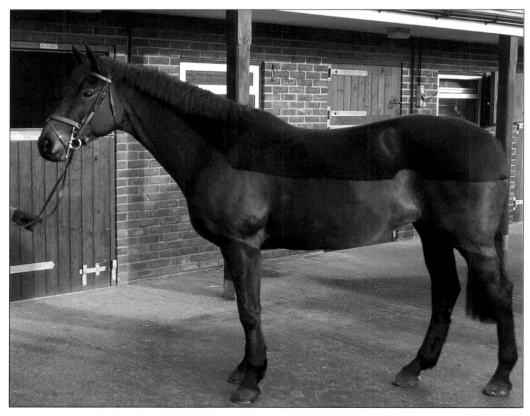

occupied. A small amount of bedding, or ideally, rubber matting on the floor, is also a good idea. Keep a feed, ready but out of sight for bribery, if necessary. You will need some chalk to mark out the clip and something solid to stand on.

It is wise to wear overalls as the hair gets everywhere and is very itchy while rubber boots and a hard hat are essential for safety. If possible, have an assistant to help you.

Your horse should be dry and as clean as possible – grease and dirt strain the motor and will blunt the blades very quickly. Ideally, he should already be accustomed to the clippers: if he isn't, get him used to the noise. Leave him in a box adjacent to other horses, then allow him to watch one of them being clipped. It that doesn't alarm him, run the clippers over him but keep them switched off. Then switch on the clippers and with your free hand touch the horse so that he can feel the vibration through your body. You will find that he slowly gets used to the idea. Don't attempt a difficult clip the first time. It can be helpful to use battery-operated clippers for the head and awkward areas or possibly the whole horse – they are not very powerful but have a smaller head and are quieter, with less vibration than standard ones. Try playing a radio or putting cotton wool in the horse's ears to drown out the sound. A twitch applied to the nose may be necessary to keep him still for his own safety but you need to have experience of using one. Tranquillizing tablets or injections may help in extreme cases but it is better to rely on kindness, patience and perhaps a little bribery in the form of some short feed.

How to clip Check the clippers are correctly assembled. The motor may be strained if the tension screw is too tight and the blades will heat up. Too loose, and they will pull rather than clip. Mark the lines of the required clip with chalk.

If well behaved, a horse can be tied up to clip, though a nervous or fidgety one will need to be held by a calm and sensible helper.

A haynet is useful to stop the horse from getting bored and fidgety but cannot be used while clipping the head and neck. Start at the shoulder and, in the case of difficult horses, leave the awkward areas until last or another occasion.

Untie the horse to clip the head. An assistant

is a help with all but the most docile animals. Steady the head and protect the eyes with your hand when clipping anywhere near them. Someone to hold a leg forward makes it much easier to slip between and around the fore-legs.

Stretch out loose areas of skin before clipping them. Check frequently that the blades are not hot, particularly when clipping the head. Clean and lubricate the blades at frequent intervals, brushing away loose hair and soaking them in a shallow tray of surgical spirit to help cool them and remove grease. Apply a light film of oil or, better still, clean and lubricate them with special clipper spray. When clipping, work against the hair and let the clippers do the work – do not push them. Never clip inside the ears, the base of the tail or the eye whiskers. Leave the nose whiskers on a

horse which lives out.

After clipping, thoroughly clean the clippers and blades and disinfect them. Before storing them, have them sharpened and smear them with petroleum jelly to prevent rusting.

Left
Clipping takes time and skill, but most people should be able to obtain a reasonable result with practice. Always wear a hard hat and be especially careful when clipping nervous or young horses.

Opposite top: A chaser clip: below: A trace clip.

Below: A blanket clip. Bottom: A full clip. In a hunter clip, an area the shape of the saddle and the legs are left unclipped.

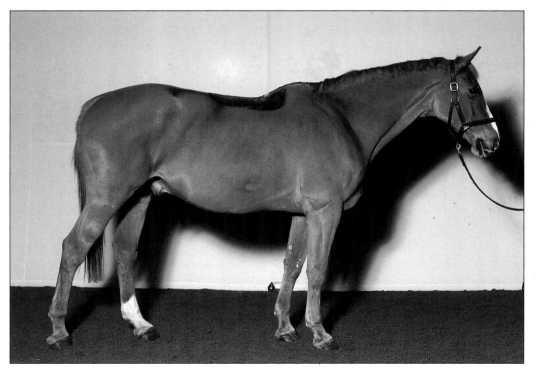

Chapter Seven
THE FOOT AND SHOEING

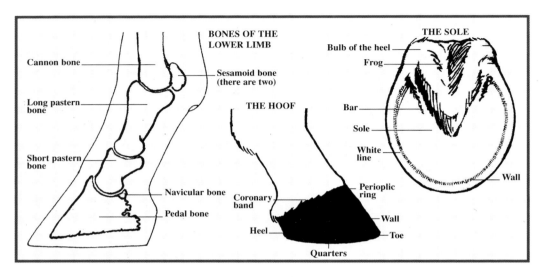

The old saying 'No foot no horse' is an adage the horse owner should never forget. Most cases of lameness originate in the foot but good stable management and shoeing can, in many instances, make a huge difference. Conformation, daily care, good nutrition and expert regular shoeing are all involved in maintaining continuing soundness.

The Structure of the Foot

The foot is relatively small for the size and weight of the horse which it must carry but through clever design manages both to resist wear and absorb concussion.

The hoof is made up of various types of horn. It is itself devoid of sensitivity but protects the sensitive structures within.

The hoof wall This grows down from the coronary band which is rather like the quick of your fingernail and stretches around the top of the hoof. The wall is insensitive and constantly growing and consists of tubes of horn bonded together which can bend and compress under pressure. This allows it to absorb concussion and means that the shape of the wall can be gradually adjusted by trimming the ground surface. It also means that the foot, if neglected, can grow out of shape. A thin layer, which looks rather like varnish, extends about two-thirds of the way down the hoof from the coronary band. Called the periople it controls the moisture content within the foot but rasping some of it away when shaping the foot probably does not cause the foot to dry out as was once feared. It usually takes between 9 and 12 months for the hoof to grow from top to bottom, but this can be considerably affected by the horse's nutrition. A sick horse or one in poor condition will produce poorer quality, slower-growing horn while access to good spring grass, for example, will produce a spurt of growth. This can

often be seen and clearly felt as parallel rings in the wall and your farrier will be able to tell you quite a lot about the state of your horse's health several months ago. Breeding is also a factor: for example, native ponies usually have strong, hard feet while Thoroughbreds often have thin crumbly horn. This can be caused by feed deficiencies and there are some good remedial supplements on the market which your vet will advise you about. Very wet or dry ground conditions will tend to make the feet correspondingly soft or brittle and prone to cracking. Wet bedding with a high ammonia content can make the horn crumbly while super-clean woodshavings will draw the feet, making them dry and hard. White feet seem to be more prone to problems than black ones.

The bars These are the continuation of the wall where it turns inwards at the heel and gradually fade away halfway down the frog. They are capable of distributing and carrying weight and so increasing the bearing surface of the foot.

The sole This covers the underside of the foot and protects the sensitive structures within. It is slightly concave which helps it to support weight. The horn of the sole varies in thickness from horse to horse. Thin-soled flat feet are more prone to bruising from hard ground and stones. Unlike the wall, excess sole tends to flake away naturally and it rarely needs more than light paring.

The frog Situated at the back of the foot, this is wedge-shaped and made of rubbery horn. It has a central cleft and one down either side. It supports and protects the internal structures and prevents the heels from contracting. Its shape also makes it an important non-slip device. The frog should only touch the ground in soft going, especially in the shod foot. Pressure on the frog causes it to expand when weight is put on the foot. This is part of a

very important **anti-concussion** device. As the foot hits the ground the weight compresses a fatty pad inside the foot down against the frog. The pressure dissipates back up and out of the foot sideways through the **lateral cartilages** of the wall and coronary band. The lateral cartilages are wing-shaped and attach to either side of the pedal bone (the main bone in the foot). You can feel the top of them above the coronary band towards the back of the foot and they should yield to thumb pressure.

The white line This is a narrow line of softer light-coloured horn where the wall and sole meet. It shows clearly the width of the wall so is very useful to the farrier when he nails on the shoe. In some situations it becomes wider and filled with crumbly horn (*see Laminitis, page 32*).

The laminae The inside of the wall of the foot is covered with thin vertical leaves of horn like the underside of a mushroom or the leaves of a book. These interlock with sensitive fleshy leaves growing from the pedal bone. The connection is very strong but still allows the wall to slide down as it grows. The horny laminae help with weight-bearing and absorb concussion.

Injuries Any damage to the coronary band will affect the growth of the wall. An example is **sandcrack** which originates as a fine crack at the coronet and widens out due to pressure towards the bottom of the hoof. **Grass cracks** on the other hand are less serious as they are splits which start at ground level, and it is easier to prevent them from extending up the hoof. They are caused by the wall splitting and breaking for various reasons, including neglect.

Grit or dirt can work its way up the white line or through cracks in the wall causing pressure on the sensitive tissues, infection and lameness.

Bruising to the sensitive structures under the sole may be caused by a stone or by hard uneven ground. A bruise in the angle between the wall and the bar is called a **corn**. It may be caused by a stone getting caught there but recurrent corns are often due to unbalanced feet with too much pressure at the back of the foot crushing the blood vessels under the sole. Leaving the shoes on for too long so that the heel of the shoe turns in and presses on the seat of corn is another common cause.

Punctures to the sole or frog may be caused by a nail or other sharp object. The hole usually closes up again straightaway but the dirt trapped inside causes infection and pus is produced. The resulting pressure leads to pain and a very lame horse. Punctures in the section of the foot from the point of the frog back to the heel are potentially dangerous as the underlying bones and associated structures may be involved.

Foot balance

Correct foot balance helps the horse remain sound and to move as well as possible. Careful trimming of the feet of foals and very young horses can actually correct gait abnormalities and encourage the horse to stand and move correctly. The aim with adult horses is to trim the foot so that it is placed to the ground as level as possible avoiding excessive stress on any one area of the foot or limb.

Foot /pastern axis From the side, the ideal angle of the fore-foot and pastern is approx 50° to the ground, the hind 55°. The angle of both the front and the back of the hoof should be the same as that of the pastern. The length of the heel should be about one-third the length of the toe. Even if the pastern is not at the ideal angle it is still important that the angle of the foot matches it.

In ideal conformation, the two halves of the ground surface of the foot should be roughly symmetrical. The distance across the widest part of the fore-feet should be the same as the length from toe to heel. This shape is good for weight-bearing (60% of the horse's weight is taken by the fore-legs). The hind-feet are slightly narrower so that they don't interfere with each other as they propel the horse forward.

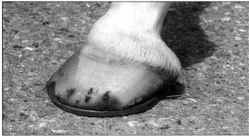

This horse has weak heels which is a conformation defect. Careful trimming and regular shoeing with a wide-webbed, long-heeled shoe (or an egg-bar shoe in bad cases) will improve the situation.

The two side walls should be the same height and at almost the same angle (the inside may be slightly more upright as it carries more weight).

It is essential that the farrier trims the feet to produce the best possible balance at every shoeing, and the toe must be cut back enough. If the interval between shoeings is too long it will be very difficult to keep the feet balanced. It can also be difficult to balance the feet of a horse which stands and moves crookedly. The farrier and vet will need to discuss together what is best for the individual animal.

Shoeing: why shoe?

Shoeing is very important in preventing excessive wear to the hooves of ridden horses, particularly on roads and abrasive surfaces such as sand and gravel. It helps protect the foot from splitting, cracking and bruising and maintains or improves the shape and balance of the feet, maximizing the horse's freedom and straightness of movement and soundness.

Horses not in work or with well-shaped, strong feet, doing little or no work on hard surfaces, will usually either not require shoeing at all or need only front shoes. Regular correct trimming

is however essential.

Horses should be shod every four to six weeks depending on hoof growth and shoe wear. More frequent shoeing may cause problems such as possible weakening and breaking up of the hoof wall with consequent loss of shoes due to the close proximity of nail holes and subsequent difficulty when re-shoeing. Shoeing less often presents problems which include shoes being cast, breaking of the wall, corns (bruising in the angle between the wall at the heel and the frog) as well as progressive deterioration of foot balance both prior to the next shoeing and in the long term.

If a shoe becomes loose you will need to re-shoe straight away. It is quite easy to recognize a shoe which is becoming loose; when the horse moves on a hard surface the loose shoe will sound different, making a 'clinking' sound.

Loss of loose shoes is not the only warning that a horse requires shoeing; look out for raised clenches; heels of the shoe turned in and pressing on the seat of a corn; a shoe worn either all over or very badly in one place (usually the toe); the hoof wall overgrowing the shoe or the hoof grown too long.

Make your farrier's life as easy as possible – book regular appointments and make sure the horse

In case of emergency and to avoid injury to the horse's foot or cuts to the opposite leg, it is useful to be able to remove a very loose shoe or one that is badly twisted (shown here and below). Make sure you are shown the safest method by a professional farrier.

is in and settled with clean, dry legs and feet. Ensure there is a place with good light and a hard smooth level surface where the farrier can work (undercover if possible).

Above all, teach your horse good manners. From the time he is a few days old, a foal can be made accustomed to having his legs touched and and his feet picked up and held. He should be introduced to the farrier at an early age. It is false economy to skimp on having a youngster's feet trimmed – if neglected he could have problems with them for the rest of his life.

Most horses accept the shoeing procedure with equanimity. However, there will always be a few that prove difficult. Young horses and those which have not been handled much need patience, time and a calm but firm approach. They may be afraid of slipping or losing their balance, especially when a hind-leg is held up. (Try a different surface and remember it is tiring to stand on three legs, so increase the time gradually and try to put the horse's leg down (gently) before he starts to pull it away from you.)

Some will be more calm and docile in their own stable, but others will be safer to handle in a larger area. Always have someone hold the horse: the handler can then give it confidence and reassurance when it might otherwise panic and pull back, if tied.

Some horses object to being restrained. They can also be anxious and may be remembering a bad experience. Others just lack obedience and manners: it is important that you can tell the difference. Generally, the progressive approach is still the right one but a stern voice or quick smack can sometimes be the answer.

There is another category of 'difficult' horse – the one that is in pain. This applies particularly to older horses and is something you should always investigate. Administer pain-killers and try to find the most comfortable angle at which to hold the leg. In severe cases, sedatives will be necessary for the sake of both horse and farrier – seek your vet's advice.

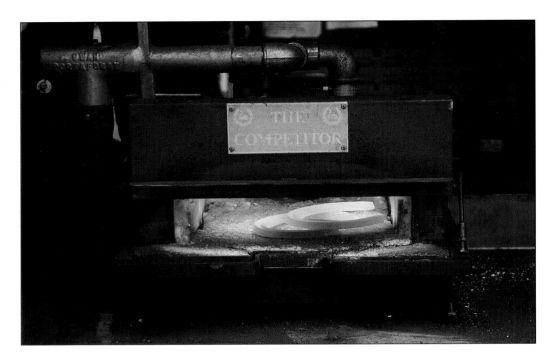

1 Above: All four shoes are removed. The farrier straightens or cuts the clenches using a buffer and hammer. He then gently levers off the shoe with pincers, starting at the heels and taking care not to break the wall. It is possible to ease the shoe, tap it back into place then withdraw the protruding nail heads one by one with the pincers. This avoids breaking the wall and the horse accidently standing on a half-removed shoe.

Hot shoeing

The horse is tied or held (an assistant should always be available) in a well-lit area with a hard, smooth surface. Unless the farrier knows the horse well he should watch it walk on level ground and note its action and current foot balance. He will also examine the pattern of wear on the existing shoes and select suitable new ones (these are usually machine-made in bulk but are occasionally made by farriers themselves) which he will heat in the forge.

The farrier will select a shoe of suitable weight, size and type. It is important that the heels of the shoe are long enough and are fitted a little wide of the wall to support the back of the foot and allow for the natural expansion of the heels. Shoeing shorter at the heels to reduce the risk of the horse pulling the shoe off is a very bad idea. If the back of the foot is not supported, too much strain is thrown onto the flexor tendons, leading to strain. Even more crucially, extra pressure is exerted on the internal structures of the back of the foot, the blood supply will be affected, and the heels will be prone to collapse. This is the perfect scenario for the development of navicular syndrome. Pain due to damage to the navicular bone and associated structures in the back of the foot is probably the commonest form of chronic lameness and good shoeing can do much to forestall or alleviate the problem.

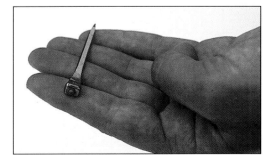

Studs Jumping studs are used to help the horse grip on grass. They are mainly used in the hind shoes but sometimes all round and are usually placed on the outside heel of the shoe. As such, they unbalance the feet badly if the ground is firm. They can be fitted in the inside as well but they may injure the horse if he brushes. They should be left in for as short a time as possible and the threaded hole kept clean, oiled and filled with cotton wool or a special plug.

Road studs are designed to prevent the horse from slipping on tarmac and have a hard tungsten core. They also unbalance the feet. A better option is to use road nails fitted towards both heels of each shoe. They slightly reduce the amount of natural give as the foot is placed to the ground but do not affect the balance and are a great help if roads are slippery.

2 Above: The foot is trimmed and balanced, removing excess wall with hoof cutters and rasp and trimming ragged pieces of frog or flaky horn with the drawing knife. The sole and frog must not be pared excessively.

Top left
Farriers can now travel to yards for hot-shoeing, with mobile forges which fit into the back of a vehicle and are fuelled by butane gas.

Centre top
Left: Hunter shoe
Right: Wide-web shoe

Centre below
Left: Egg-bar shoe
Right: Straight-bar shoe

Left
Road nails are used for horses doing a lot of work on hard surfaces. They help the horse to grip the road.

3 Above: The shoes are heated in the forge and shaped on the anvil with a hammer. A pritchel is used to carry the hot shoe.

4 Above: The hot shoe is briefly applied to the hoof to test for fit and to check for a smooth bearing surface, raised portions of wall being more charred. Young or nervous horses may be 'smoke shy' in which case the shoe can be partially cooled in a bucket of water. Care should then be taken not to apply it for too long.

5 Below: The shoe is adjusted, as necessary, using hammer and anvil. It is checked again, and immersed in cold water.

6 Above: The shoe is nailed on with the minimum number of nails that will hold it firmly, commonly four on the outside and three on the inside. A cracked or broken hoof wall should be avoided and nails should not be driven too near the heels as this would prevent the normal expansion of the hoof.

Above: *The farrier likes to build up a good relationship with his regular customers and most horses will stand quietly throughout the process.*

7 Above: After each nail is driven home, the sharp end is twisted off with the claw of the driving hammer and the shoe is then tightened and the clenches created by placing the pincers under each nail stub while the head is hammered.

8 Above: The clenches are shaped with the rasp and turned and bedded using clenching tongs or hammer and pincers. The clenches and the lower edge of the wall where it adjoins the shoe are lightly smoothed with the rasp. The horse is trotted up to check for soundness.

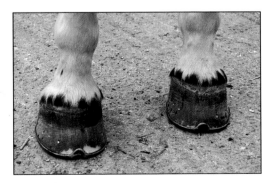

The finished result. This horse's feet are not really a pair and toe-in. The farrier is gradually correcting them to improve their balance and symmetry. The shoeing procedure may vary in sequence, particularly if the farrier has an apprentice who can remove shoes and finish off. When cold shoeing (without a forge), the basic procedure is the same but the adjustment possible to the shoe is quite limited. Hot shoeing enables a more accurate and secure fit. However, a good farrier shoeing cold is preferable to an indifferent one shoeing hot.

Chapter Eight
SADDLERY, BOOTS AND RUGS

Your horse's tack is of vital importance to him as well as to your own safety: it is also very expensive. Therefore it is important that you make the right choice, particularly where saddles are concerned. Before selecting one, ask yourself what your main objectives are. A general-purpose saddle can be used for flat work, jumping, and is the most comfortable for hacking. However, if dressage or jumping are the most important aspects of your horse's work it is worth buying a special saddle for the job.

Badly-fitting tack can have a detrimental effect on your horse's well-being and way of going. An ill-fitting saddle can cause severe back problems, and even lameness.

Choosing and fitting a bit Comfort and control are your two main objectives when selecting a bit. Horses often pull away from pain and a horse fighting discomfort is hardly likely to be attentive or co-operative.

The search for comfort can be divided into three areas: the design of the bit, the fit of the bit, and the rider's hands. Horses' mouths vary considerably in their shape and sensitivity, so it is important to choose a bit which is physically comfortable for that particular animal. The bit must be of the right width to fit correctly in the right place in the horse's mouth. The bit is a tool for conveying the rider's wishes to his mount, so the rider's ability is of paramount importance. Unsteady, clumsy rein aids will cause the least discomfort if the bit is mild. The more severe or complicated the bit, the more sensitivity and skill is required. Control in crudest terms is the ability to stop, start, turn and select a speed at will. There should, however, be far more to it than this. The horse must of course react to the rider's aids, but the choice of bit should reflect the quality of those aids and the level of schooling of the horse so that he is able to accept the influence of the bit with the minimum resistance and work confidently in harmony with his rider.

To complement the bit, there are various nosebands, martingales and other schooling aids which require the same degree of care in their selection. In a perfect world, none of these would be necessary. In practice, they can be very useful if correctly used but can cause all sorts of problems when abused.

The horse's mouth The teeth of the upper jaw are wider apart than those of the lower. As a result, when the horse grinds his food, sharp edges form on the outside of the upper molars and the inside of the lower ones. In addition, hooks often form on the end of the first upper and last lower molars. These will be more marked if the horse has a slight

'parrot mouth' which is fairly common. Sharp teeth will prevent the horse chewing his food efficiently and can be a cause of loss of condition. Tilting his head to one side as he eats, or dropping food out of his mouth, known as 'quidding', are typical indications of this problem. Sharp teeth can also cause great discomfort when the horse is ridden, in bad cases actually lacerating the insides of the cheeks or damaging the tongue. Rasping the molar teeth regularly (it doesn't hurt!) will remove any sharp points or hooks. Bitting problems can also be caused by 'wolf tooth'. These are tiny shallow-rooted teeth situated just in front of the first upper molars. They can interfere with the action of the bit and cause the horse some discomfort, especially if they are loose. Removing them can be done simply and quickly if they are suspected of causing problems (*see Dentistry, page 34*). Signs of discomfort include head-shaking, over-reacting to the rein aids, tilting the head to one side, refusing to accept contact with the rider's hands, or leaning heavily on one rein. Variations in the head and jaw shape will affect the horse's comfort and response to the bit. For example, narrow, thinly-covered bars will be very sensitive, thick fleshy ones less so. A tongue that is large for the size of mouth may make an apparently mild, thick bit too much of a mouthful. This can be made worse if a tight noseband further restricts the space available. A short distance between the incisor teeth and the molars (made worse if the horse has tushes) can mean there is just not enough room for the two bits of a double bridle.

How the bit works
The mouthpiece Thick ones are milder than thin ones (try carrying a heavy weight in a thin-

handled bag). Smooth ones are mild, those with squared-off edges, ridges or twists, more severe. Rollers discourage strong horses from taking hold of the bit. Mouthpieces covered in rubber, vulcanite, nylon and similar synthetics are mild. The very soft pliable ones are particularly so, but also chewable. Copper and sweet iron encourage the horse to salivate and are warmer than stainless steel. Hollow mouths are lighter and the horse can more easily play with them than with solid bits. A slightly curved one (mullen-mouth) allows more room for the tongue than a straight bar.

The rings or **cheeks** Eggbutts, or fixed rings and fixed cheeks on curb bits, discourage movement. Loose rings and sliding cheek curbs encourage playing with the bit and salivation. Large rings or cheeks and bit guards help prevent a bit from being pulled through the mouth.

Most bits these days are made either all or partly of stainless steel which is strong and looks good. Nickel is unsuitable as it is too soft and bends and wears easily.

Snaffles These may be jointed, straight or mullen-mouth. There are many different types from very mild through strong to severe. A mild version is usually considered the most suitable bit for a young horse or inexperienced rider. To say a horse is 'snaffle-mouthed' is a commendation inferring that it is well mannered and does not pull. In general, it should be possible with correct schooling to train any horse to go well in a simple snaffle. This is reflected in the dressage rules which require horses competing at preliminary and novice levels to wear simple snaffles with smooth mouthpieces.

The bit acts mainly on the corners of the mouth. The mullen-mouth variety places some pressure on the tongue while the jointed mouthpiece creates a squeezing 'nutcracker' effect on the mouth and as such has a stronger action. Despite this, a great many horses are very happy with it. The double-jointed 'French link' lessens this effect and should not be confused with the 'Doctor Bristol' which is a quite strong, though not severe, bit. Snaffle bits are described as having a head-raising effect.

Double bridle This is a more complicated system of bitting and should not be used until the horse works well in a snaffle bridle. The rider needs to be able to use the two reins independently of one another and with great sensitivity. It is mainly used for advanced dressage and in the show ring. It should be used to add finesse to the horse's performance and not to force his head into place or as 'brakes' as is unfortunately sometimes the

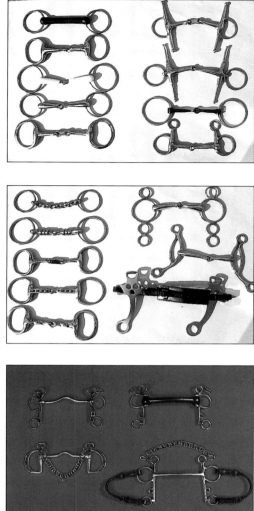

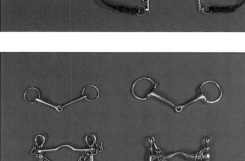

case. The bridoon acts in the same way as a snaffle while the curb encourages flexion at the poll and jaw by a combination of pressure on the bars, poll and chin groove. The tongue is taken up into the upward bend in the mouthpiece (a tongue groove if shallow, a port if larger) allowing the bit to press on the bars to a greater or lesser extent. The longer the cheeks of the bit, the more severe it is. To avoid resistance, horses need to be taught gently in walk or even in hand to relax their jaws when they feel the pressure of a curb chain.

Fitting a double bridle The bridoon is fitted like a snaffle (possibly a little higher). The slip head fastens on the offside. Start with about 2½ cm (1 inch) between the two mouthpieces at the lips, adjusting if necessary and checking that the bridoon is lying above the curb in the mouth, that the bits are well clear of the tushes, and that the curb chain rests comfortably in the chin groove. The curb chain should come into action when the cheeks are at an angle of approximately 45° with the lips. It must be absolutely smooth with no twists.

Pelham These bits are attempting to do the job of a double bridle but with one mouthpiece. The action is at best indistinct but seems to suit quite a lot of horses, encouraging them to flex and improving control while usually employing a relatively mild mullen-mouthpiece. They are quite often used in the show ring for horses who, for whatever reason, are not happy in a double bridle. One disadvantage is that horses do tend to learn to over-bend or lean on them. They can more easily be used by a less experienced rider and leather couplings can be attached to the bit so that it can be used with one rein, if necessary, although this further reduces any subtlety of action.

The gag These are strong bits designed for horses that pull hard with their heads down. They are an adaptation of the snaffle and will be more or less severe depending on the thickness of the mouthpiece. They work by exerting simultaneous downward pressure on the poll and strong upward pressure on the corners of the mouth which produces a clear head-raising effect. It is a good idea to attach a second rein directly to the rings for

Top
A selection of mild snaffle bits.

Second from top
(Left) More severe snaffle bits, increasing in severity from top to bottom. (Right) Two examples of gag snaffles. (Below) A bitless bridle.

Third from top
A selection of pelhams and a kimblewick (bottom left).

Above
A selection of double bridle bits.

Right
A snaffle bridle with flash noseband and buckled jumping reins with martingale stops. Well-designed, good-quality tack will last longer and is stronger than cheaper versions.

use when the horse is not pulling, as continuous use can tend to lock the horse into a hollow outline.

The bitless bridle These combine pressure on the nose and chin groove to provide a deceptively strong means of control. They are useful for a horse with a temporarily damaged mouth but are most often used for animals which seriously dislike a conventional bit. Sometimes a horse which continually fights and tries to run away from rein contact, will relax and become a different animal in one of these. They still require sensitive hands and must be fitted carefully

Choosing a bit for your horse Aim for the mildest which your horse will respect and which is comfortable for his mouth-shape. Whether you are starting from scratch, or trying to solve a problem, always start with a mild bit, progressing to a different type or one of greater severity only if really necessary.

How do you know he is comfortable? Does he look at ease, holding the bit quietly or gently chomping it with a wet mouth (salivating) but not anxiously fussing or foaming. He should respond to the rein aids promptly but not abruptly with a steady head carriage and a relaxed jaw (the jaws should be slightly parted rather than clamped shut, open wide or 'crossed' in resistance). A horse who tries to get his tongue over the bit, draws the tongue back, or lolls it out to the side, may be telling you that he needs more space for his tongue or that he dislikes the feel of the mouthpiece. Fitting the bit too low will also teach the horse he can get his tongue over it, which can quickly become a habit. If you sense that all is not well, check for physical damage. As well as problems due to sharp teeth, the bars could be bruised, or the corners of the mouth bruised, sore, or even split. Causes may be clumsy or rough riding or a too-thin or worn bit. A dry-mouthed horse will be more prone to soreness. The bit cheeks or rings may rub the sides of the face around the corners of

the mouth if the fit or shape of bit is not quite right, the rider's hands unsteady, or the horse stiff to one rein. Rubs to the back of the jaw may occur if the horse resists the curb chain constantly or if it is fitted too tight or too high so that it lies over the bone rather than resting in the curb groove.

Try to look behind any problem to the root cause. Is the horse uncomfortable in his mouth, causing him to pull and fight, or just badly schooled with no idea how to accept a soft contact with the rider's hand. This is where an experienced second opinion can be of great help. Don't forget that a change of noseband, a martingale or other schooling aid may be the answer rather than a different bit. A stronger bit is no substitute for correct schooling and can often make matters worse. Control, however, is essential and if, for example, a normally well-mannered animal gets over-enthusiastic when galloping across country, it is better to use a stronger bit quietly than to haul on a mild one. This also applies to children on

Left
A correctly fitted double bridle. Make sure the curb chain is not twisted as this could cause discomfort.

Below
A Western-style bridle looking stunning on this beautiful cream saddle-bred horse.

Opposite top
A general-purpose saddle. This is a compromise: when schooling on the flat, it allows the rider to sit comfortably, but is cut sufficiently forward for jumping over small fences.

Opposite centre
A straight-cut, deep-seated dressage saddle.

Opposite bottom
A jumping saddle. The longer seat and forward-cut flap and knee rolls help the rider sit in balance when jumping.

ponies. A small child on a strong pony will learn to yank and pull while a stronger bit will enable the child to ride with a light hand and most of all stay safely in control.

The bridle These are made in sizes to fit most breeds of horses and ponies. When fitting a bridle, observe the following: the buckles of a correctly fitted bridle should not be set on the first or last holes as this leaves no room for adjustment and looks less smart. The browband must be large enough or the headpiece will rub the base of the ears; it must not be adjusted too high so that it rubs the ears or too low which looks untidy and pulls the bridle out of position.

There should be four fingers' width between the throatlash and jawbone and two fingers' width between the cavesson noseband and the nose. The noseband should be halfway between the corners of the mouth and the angle of the cheek-bone.

Nosebands The *cavesson noseband* is primarily for appearance. In addition, a standing martingale can be attached to it. It should be fitted halfway between the cheek-bones and the corners of the lips and you should be able to get two fingers between the noseband and the jaw.

A *drop noseband* is for a horse who tries to evade the bit by opening its mouth wide or crossing the jaws. The noseband discourages this by exerting pressure on the nose and chin groove. Take special care that it does not interfere with the breathing. It should fit just below the end of the nasal bone, roughly four fingers above the nostrils. The bottom strap should fit snugly but not unduly tightly under the bit.

The *flash noseband* has a similar effect to the *drop* but puts pressure on the nose a little higher up; it has the advantage that you can fit a standing martingale to the *cavesson* section. Both parts should fit snugly but not tightly. The *cavesson* should be slightly higher than usual but be careful that it doesn't rub the cheek-bones. The *drop* strap fits under the bit.

The *grakle* is a stronger noseband and suitable for horses that pull. It is often used by cross-country riders but is not allowed in pure dressage competitions. It discourages the horse from crossing his jaw, applying stronger localized pressure on the nose where the straps intersect. It is adjusted higher than the *drop* and so is less likely to interfere with the breathing of a galloping horse. Both straps should be snugly fitted, the top one just below the corner of the cheek-bones with the bottom under the bit, though the position can vary.

Reins The reins must be long enough, reaching easily to the withers when the horse's head and neck are fully extended. If too long, the rider or horse may get a foot through them.

Fitting the bridle First put the headcollar on the horse and tie it up. Select a suitable bridle and undo all the keepers and runners. Untie the horse and hold on to the rope, but gently, so as not to

alarm him. Hold the bridle up to the horse's head to measure it. Adjust the cheekpieces. Try the bridle on, but stop immediately if it is much too big or too tight. Re-adjust if necessary. Tidy the horse's forelock and check position of the browband. Next check the height of the bit; for a jointed bit you should see one to two wrinkles in the corner of the mouth and for a mullen or straight bar one wrinkle. The bit is correctly fitted if, when pulled down gently, it leaves no gap.

In some cases the bit will need to be fitted a little higher to discourage the horse from getting his tongue over it, but it should never make him 'smile'.

Check the width of the bit; if too narrow it may pinch, if too wide it will tend to drag through the mouth and rub the lips or the side of the face; a 6-mm (¼-inch) space each side is about right.

Fasten the throatlash; you should allow a hand's width between it and the side of the cheek. It should be quite loose to allow the horse to flex easily. Finally, fasten the noseband inside the cheekpieces.

Saddle fitting Never underestimate the extent to which the fit of a horse's saddle can affect his performance.

Correct fit can also affect the rider. A comfortable saddle of the right type will make a big difference to position, balance and effectiveness. A good saddler is trained to fit the saddle for you. The main requirements are these: for the horse, the saddle should keep the spine completely free of pressure and the gusset should be the correct width along its full length with little or no tapering towards the cantle. It should offer as large a bearing surface as possible to spread the rider's weight. It must also match the curve of the horse's back and the contours of his muscles to prevent uneven pressure, pinching or restriction of movement, rocking (up, down, or from side-to-side), and slipping forward or back.

For the rider, the right seat size and the correct length flap for the rider's thighs are important.

If the rider is large for the horse, it is better to use a longer saddle for the rider's comfort and to spread their weight. Bear in mind that if the saddle is very long it may press on the horse's loins and risk bruising the kidneys. The saddle should distribute the rider's weight evenly and allow him to sit in balance, tipped neither forward nor back.

No one design of saddle will fit every horse. Be prepared to try a variety to find as near as possible a perfect fit.

A young horse just starting work or one in poor condition will greatly change shape as its muscles develop and weight changes.

The saddle flocking can be adjusted to some degree but a different saddle may be necessary. Don't be tempted to start with a makeshift saddle on a young horse. The extra cost of ensuring a horse's comfort at this formative stage is a long-term investment.

Old horses, and those that have been working in a hollow outline, can be lacking in muscle

comfortable than new ones as they have already been 'worked in'. Always have them checked by a saddler for condition or possible damage to the tree: to some extent saddles do mould themselves to a particular horse's shape. It is important that you don't just sit on the saddle; try riding in all three paces and if necessary over jumps. *When putting the saddle on, place it a little too far forward and then slide it gently into position, checking for fit and comfort.* The angle of the 'points' of the tree and the general shape of the front of the panel should conform to the contours of the horse's side and should not pinch or gape over or behind the shoulders.

The girth should fall naturally into the girth groove behind the elbow or it will pull the saddle out of position when tightened. Never leave a horse unattended, even briefly, when it is wearing a saddle with the girth unsecured.

Maintenance A new saddle may need reflocking after only a few weeks, otherwise yearly checks are sensible. The flocking may have become compressed, causing the saddle to drop too low on the horse's back and affect the balance. The panels may also become lumpy or uneven. Daily and weekly checks will bring to notice any loose or worn stitching or damage which needs immediate attention.

around the saddle area, particularly behind the withers. These horses can be difficult to fit and a thickly padded numnah may well be necessary.

If you choose to use other than a very thin numnah, make sure you check that the saddle still fits. There is no point in the saddler carefully fitting your saddle only for you to add inches of padding, making it too tight or altering its balance.

Second-hand saddles can be initially more

Checking Tack for Safety

Bridle
Check the condition of the leather, especially wear points around the bit and under buckles. Check the stitching, particularly around buckles and billets, that holes are not stretched or worn and that billet hooks are not loose and are correctly fastened. Check condition of the reins, particularly those made of rubber or webbing, and that the bit has no sharp edges where the mouthpiece and rings join.

Saddle
Check for a cracked or broken tree – there should be no excessive movement when pommel and cantle are flexed towards each other: there should be no give in the front arch and no creaking when in use; a sudden drop low onto the withers is a warning sign. Thoroughly check stitching, especially the top of the girth straps and stirrup leathers; check both sides and that the holes are not stretched or worn. The condition of the leather should be supple, well oiled and not cracked, especially girth straps and stirrup leathers. Check where the leather runs through the stirrup irons.

Make sure the catch on the stirrup bar is down and that the bar is not too tight or too loose. Stirrups should be made of stainless steel with suitable rubber treads.

Check the girth – it should be in perfect condition.

Fitting a running martingale This discourages the horse from lifting his head too high and so offers the rider more control. The neck-strap buckles fasten on the left and should follow the front line of the shoulder. The strap to the girth passes through the front legs and should allow freedom of chest and leg movements without hanging too low (approximately 10 cm (4 inches) when pulled down). It joins to the neck-strap at the base of the neck and is held by a rubber ring where the leather divides, each strap having a ring through which the rein passes.

There should be no interference with the rein action unless the horse carries his head too high when the martingale will exert a downward pull on the mouth. The reins must be fitted with rubber stops between the bit and the martingale rings; this is essential to prevent the rings catching on a billet, buckle or tooth.

Standing martingale This prevents the horse's head from being carried or thrown too high by pressure on the nose. It should be fitted in the same way as the running martingale but the main strap attaches to a cavesson noseband adjusted so that it can just be pushed up into the throat.

Breast plate This prevents the saddle from slipping backwards and to an extent from sliding sideways. It should be fitted in the same way as a running martingale. The straps from the top of the hunting-style breast plate should be attached to the 'D's screwed on to the front of the saddle. You can add martingale attachments to this type. The racing type attaches to the girth straps. The whole thing should allow freedom of movement without being so loose as to be ineffective.

Tack Cleaning

This is not everyone's favourite task but it is important and should not be skimped.

Tack is expensive. The better it is looked after the longer it will last. Rain, sun, sweat and mud dry out leather and cause it to crack and possibly split. For safety's sake, dirt and sweat need to be removed and the leather softened and 'fed' with saddle soap; a suitable oil or leather treatment should be periodically applied.

The horse's comfort is the other prime concern. Stiff, hard leather and dirty numnahs or girths will quickly lead to sores. Supple leatherwork is also more comfortable for the rider (as you will know if you have ever tried riding on a shiny, stiff saddle).

Finally, well-cleaned tack looks good and is a compliment to your horse.

Daily Wash bit and stirrup irons. Wipe over leatherwork to remove grease and mud; apply saddle soap. Brush numnahs and fabric girths. Leave to dry/air as necessary.

Weekly Strip (take apart) tack. Clean thoroughly and inspect for wear. If the tack is very dry, apply an oily preparation especially designed for saddlery. Allow it to soak in before applying saddle soap and polish any metalwork, avoiding the mouthpiece of the bit; alternatively, simply buff with a cloth. Wash numnahs and fabric parts in a non-biological soap powder.

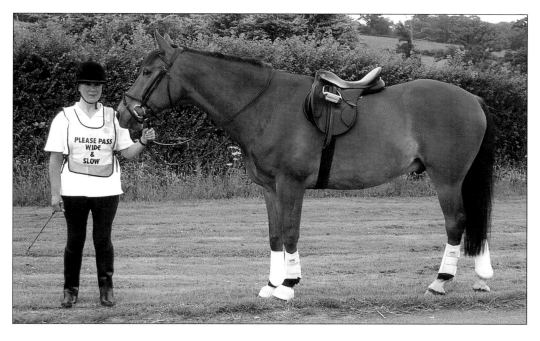

Use warm, rather than hot water, and avoid over-wetting leather. Remove grease and mud from leather with a damp sponge. When thoroughly clean, dry with a chamois leather. Wash all metalwork, rinse and dry. If leather is new, stiff and dry or has been out in the rain, neatsfoot oil or a proprietary brand will help soften it. Lightly apply with a brush or sponge, mostly on the inner 'flesh' side of the leather as this is the more absorbent. Finally, apply saddle soap with a damp sponge, massaging it into the leather.

Above
Selecting appropriate saddlery is most important as mistakes can be expensive in terms of both the horse's comfort and the owner's purse. Always seek expert advice when fitting saddles and bridles.

Left
This grey is at a rodeo show wearing Western-style saddlery which is highly decorative and looks great.

Opposite top
Your tack-room should be cool, dry and secure and a burglar alarm is advisable. These bridles have been correctly 'put up' after cleaning.

Opposite centre
Certain checks can be made to see if a saddle has sufficient clearance above the horse's back, although expert advice should always be sought before purchasing or fitting a new saddle.

Opposite below
Tack should be regularly and thoroughly cleaned and all straps and stitching checked for soundness.

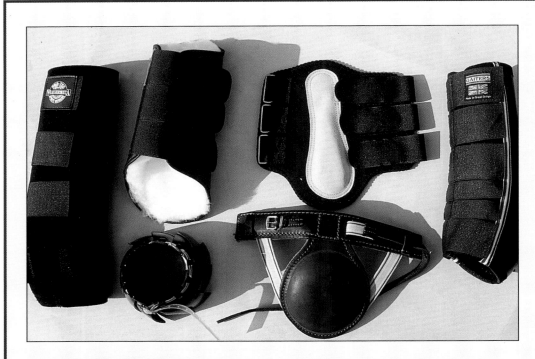

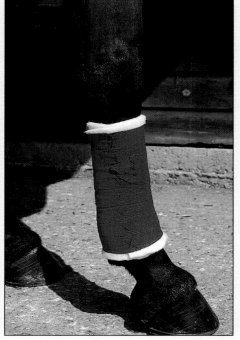

Work-boots and bandages

It is most important when working your horse, and even hacking, that his legs have adequate protection. Boots come in all shapes and sizes and all do different jobs. They should fit properly, but check that they are not too tight top and bottom when they could cause pressure ridges.

Left, from far left clockwise
Sports-boot, offering particular support to the tendons; fleece-lined brushing-boot; leather-padded brushing-boot; neoprene gaiter, which protects the back of the fetlock; exercise knee-boot, for protection when a horse stumbles;'petal' over-reach boot.

Centre left
Over-reach boot are particularly useful when jumping or engaged in fast work. They protect the heels of the fore-feet from injury when struck with the hind shoes. Many feel that they are risky used cross-country as the horse could trip himself up by treading on them. The pull-on variety are most secure.

Below
A correctly applied exercise bandage: these support and protect the lower leg and flexor tendons. They must be applied over padding or special tendon protectors. The bandages should be firm enough to give support and not slip, but not too tight when they can cause considerable damage to the tendons. Bandage and tapes (if used) should be completely smooth and tied centrally on the outside to prevent the knot pressing on the cannon bone or the tendons. For fast work, electrical tape wound over the bandage gives extra security but is not waterproof. Sewing the bandage (shown here) is preferable and will prevent it from unravelling, keeping it securely in place.

Above
Brushing-boots are possibly the most widely used form of protective boot and can be used on all four legs. Their purpose is to protect the legs from injury when they brush together. Young and unbalanced horses, and those whose action is not straight, are more likely to brush.

Right
Tendon-boots are designed to support and protect the flexor tendons during fast work The open-fronted type are designed for riders who prefer their horses to be aware when they knock a fence.

Rugs

A well-fitting rug will be shaped to the contours of the horse's shoulders and back and be deep enough to cover the belly and reach to the top of the tail. It should allow the shoulders to move freely.

For everyday and night-time use, the traditional jute rug has been largely replaced by synthetic, fibre-filled rugs made from modern lightweight materials which are comfortable and washable. Cross-over surcingles, leg-straps, and elastic surcingles are all ways of keeping the rug in place without placing undue pressure on the horse's spine.

Keep your horse warm enough but don't over-rug as horses dislike being hot. Check his ears for warmth first thing in the morning or last thing at night: if cold, he may require another rug.

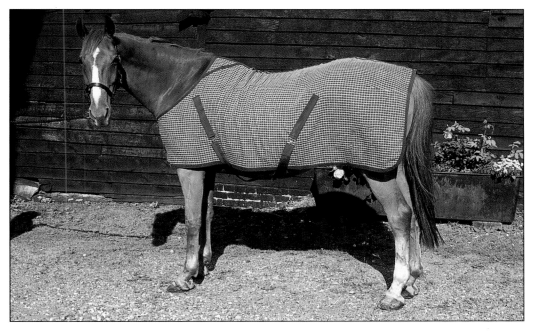

Above
The sweat sheet is a loosely woven cotton rug, rather like a string vest. It should be used in conjunction with a light over-rug to allow the horse to dry off without chilling. This rug is possibly a little big in the neck. A roller should be used if the horse is to be left unattended.

Left top
This gold, red and black-striped English Witney looks handsome and will keep a horse warm in his stable. In this case, the roller is fitted too far forward and should have a thick pad underneath to protect the horse's back.

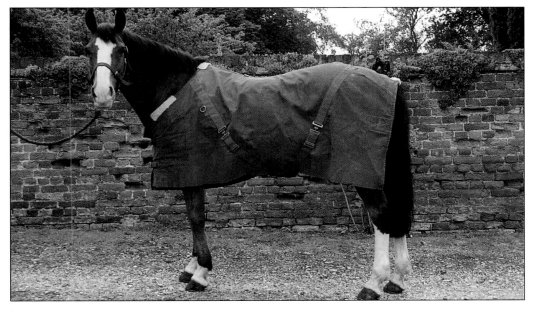

Centre
The summer sheet is manufactured from light cotton and has cross-over surcingles. It is useful in hot weather for protecting horses from flies and keeping the coat smooth.

Left
The New Zealand rug is for outdoor use and was traditionally made of canvas. However, it is now made in a variety of waterproof fabrics. It is essential for a horse who lives out to have two of these so that he always has a dry one in reserve. In very cold weather an under-rug should also be used.

Chapter Nine
BUYING A HORSE

Before deciding to purchase a horse or pony of your own, there are many factors to be realistically considered. Most important is the amount of time you have at your disposal. Keeping a horse takes up a great deal of time: are you prepared to dedicate mornings and evenings and a good chunk of your weekend to caring for him? Check your finances: keeping a horse can be very expensive whether you opt for full livery or decide to do-it-yourself.

Ask yourself why you wish to own a horse: how much enjoyment do you expect to get from a relationship with an animal? Are you prepared for the more unpleasant tasks connected with caring for him as well as the excitement of riding him for pleasure or competition?

It is unrealistic to expect young children to look after their own ponies and older ones, however keen, will have study and school commitments. Children of any age will need plenty of practical support, supervision and

Top
Heavy breeds or types can be great all-rounders as well as having strength and sturdiness. It is essential for heavy riders to have a horse that is up to weight.

Above
The Thoroughbred has great stamina, speed and grace, but is less hardy than other breeds. Only the experienced should consider buying one as they demand dedication and attention. Though highly-strung, they can, however, be most rewarding.

encouragement, even if their ponies are to be kept at livery.

Make sure in advance that you have somewhere suitable to keep the animal, can afford the added expense of tack, rugs, equipment and insurance, and have the support and advice of an experienced person.

Consider these points: what type, breed, size and build of horse is suitable for you? Native ponies and their crosses are tough, versatile and relatively cheap and easy to keep but can be strong

and wilful unless well schooled. (Shetland ponies are a typical example.)

Thoroughbreds and 'quality' horses with a lot of Thoroughbred blood may be too sharp and sensitive for all but the most experienced riders and handlers. Moreover, they will fail to thrive in less than ideal conditions and will require winter stabling.

Arabs and their crosses are fairly hardy with kind temperaments. They are generally intelligent and range from lazy to highly-strung. Ideal for endurance riding and versatile in other areas, despite their reputation, they can jump well if properly schooled.

Warm-bloods vary in build but have plenty of substance. Mostly calm and self-possessed, they often have great talent for dressage and show-jumping but may lack enthusiasm and require a strong, effective rider. They tend to lack speed and boldness cross-country. Those with a greater infusion of Thoroughbred in them tend to be more active and forward-thinking.

Many a mixed breed of one-half to three-quarters Thoroughbred would be ideal for the average amateur owner, particularly if they combine good looks and movement with some 'colder' or pony blood.

An animal that is too large or powerfully built may be too strong or difficult for a small rider to keep balanced and active, particularly if its conformation is 'on the forehand' with a thick neck and heavy front end. If it is too broad it will be unsuitable for a small child and may cause hip/back problems in a slightly-built person. A slightly tall animal, if not too strong or long in the back, is less of a problem.

Ability to carry its rider's weight is more important than height (if in doubt ask your vet), but a long-legged rider may feel insecure or foolish on a small animal.

If you intend to show or show-jump, check the horse or pony is the correct height for the classes you wish to enter. It is wise to obtain a life height certificate or confirmation of its vital statistics if they are very close to the limit.

Smooth, free paces and good natural balance are desirable, but avoid big elastic movement unless you are sure you can sit to it.

Check the horse's conformation and paces *(This is covered in more depth in Chapter One.)* These should at least be workmanlike and basically correct with sufficiently straight movement to avoid obvious brushing or strain on the joints. Look for a kind, alert and intelligent expression. Avoid animals obviously lacking in proportion such as those with a heavy forehand and weak hindquarters, the body too heavy for the limbs, or one limb turning in or out.

Above
Arabs are hardy and make great endurance horses. This gelding is 26 years young.
They are usually kind and intelligent but some can be a little lively and scatter-brained.

Left
This Suffolk Punch cross Thoroughbred is an enthusiastic all-rounder.

Lower left
This horse is seven-eighths Thoroughbred and is a great all-rounder. Such an animal tends to be hardier than a pure-bred, but still retains much of the Thoroughbred's grace and elegance.

Below
When choosing a pony for a child, it is vital that it is safe and reliable. Native breeds, such as this Dartmoor, are very hardy, need little feeding, and will happily live out all year round.

Piggy eyes are said to denote a lack of generosity but there is always the exception to the rule. Avoid feet which are not a pair or are very boxy or too flat. Avoid choosing a horse that has a very upright shoulder, very upright or angled limbs, and a long, weak back.

Also avoid a horse with a very thick neck or poorly-set head on the neck. Look for signs of previous injuries or wear and tear such as brushing scars, thickened flexor tendons, pronounced windgalls or very thickened joints.

If the horse is destined for competition work, correct, sound conformation becomes of even greater importance, but many plain animals nevertheless perform well. For showing, look for a well-made horse with quality and presence, straight, free action and no blemishes.

Your vet will advise you on conformation and any potential problems likely to arise as a result of faults or old injuries. However, he can only give a qualified opinion.

Cobs are hardy, strong and great all-rounders. They are capable of living out all-year-round and are an excellent family choice.

Right
A horse's age can be gauged by looking at its teeth which change year by year until it is 7 years old. After this, judgement becomes more approximate.

Opposite above
Choose a horse that is the correct size for you and one with which you are compatible. Being over- or under-horsed can ruin your pleasure. These two are well-matched and well on the way to developing a great relationship.

Opposite below
Before deciding to purchase, ride the horse in all paces in an arena before attempting more open spaces. It is a good idea to see the owner ride it first in order to check that the horse is safe before trying it out yourself.

Age

Young horses should not be in full work until they are four years old. A four- or five-year-old that has already 'done a lot', particularly jumping, may show signs of strain at a later date.

Pairing a young or inexperienced horse with a similar rider can be a recipe for disaster. A seven- to nine-year-old is ideal for the less experienced rider as the horse should by then be in its prime and settled into its work. An older horse, if fit and sound, can also give many years of pleasure.

When buying a foal or youngster, work out the full cost of keeping it in terms of time as well as money until it is old enough to ride. You may need assistance with its training: bear in mind that it could get injured (it will need particularly safe grazing and company all-year-round) or it may just not turn out as you had hoped. On the other hand, you will know its history, have ample time to develop a rapport and hopefully teach it good manners and sociable behaviour. Be warned against spoiling your 'baby' and ending up with a badly misbehaved, difficult-to-train animal. Value depends on looks and performance and this will tend to drop from the age of ten years onwards.

Temperament (in hand and ridden) This is possibly the single most important factor. A wonderfully kind and generous personality may well outweigh many imperfections with regard to conformation, age, type, etc.

Children and novice adults should never be tempted to buy an animal which appears ideal in all respects apart from its suspect temperament.

A person experienced in the ways of horses

may well be able to improve behaviour that is due to poor handling and riding or an unsuitable environment, but should be wary of purchasing an animal that is either clearly ungenerous or highly nervous or one that has entrenched behavioural problems or vices that could be dangerous, e.g. one that is nervous in traffic, liable to kick or bite, nap or rear; do not be tempted, even if the horse is otherwise talented and the price competitive.

Level of training Good basic schooling is important for safety and comfort even if you only intend to hack out. Avoid a horse that needs 'bringing on' or is badly schooled unless you have plenty of time, knowledge and ability.

Ideally, choose an animal suited to your present ability but with scope for improvement and development. A 'schoolmaster' with a generous temperament, and who knows the job, will put up with a lack of ability and finesse on the part of his rider. Avoid buying a lazy, insensitive animal, as even the most timid rider will find this ultimately disheartening. Look for a horse whose enthusiasm mirrors and complements your own.

A sensitive, highly-schooled animal may become badly confused, neurotic and difficult to control if ridden by a novice. A horse used to very strong, effective riding may quickly learn to take advantage of a weaker or less skilled rider.

Do not give in to vanity by over-horsing yourself, even if you intend to have lots of lessons. Remember, a horse or pony doing plenty of regular work, e.g. in a riding school, may become much livelier and naughtier when ridden lightly, or nappy when ridden without company.

There may be a genuine reason for a horse being in poor condition or recently returned to work after a long rest, but bear in mind that most horses are calmer when underfed and some may only show unsoundness when in full work.

Price Find out the level of prices current for the type of horse or pony you have in mind. This will vary from place to place and tend to be higher in late spring and early summer.

Many vendors expect to have the price 'knocked down' a little. If tack and rugs are included, check they are of good quality, fit properly, and are worth the extra money. Your vet may be willing to comment on the value for money of a particular horse.

A horse is usually cheap for a reason. It is possible that the owner does not realize its true worth or merely wishes to facilitate a quick sale, but more often than not there will be something wrong with it.

Where to look Private advertisements are to be found in horse magazines, local newspapers, saddlers and local stable yards. A reputable dealer, preferably one who has been recommended, will do their best to match you with a suitable horse but is unlikely to know anything of its past history. Beware of the 'we'll always exchange it' policy. An unscrupulous dealer may sell you an unsuitable animal in the hope of part-exchanging it for one of a series of more expensive ones.

opinion may or may not concur with your own so be prepared to go and look and possibly make many unsatisfactory journeys. If long distances are involved, photographs and videos are sometimes exchanged.

Here is a list of useful questions to ask:
- What is the reason for the sale?
- Is the horse warranted (free from vices, sound, etc.) – more likely from a sale or dealer than a private owner.
- Is the horse open to any vet?
- Is it registered with a breed society or to compete?
- Is it easy to handle, catch, box, shoe, clip?
- Is it 100 per cent safe in traffic?
- Does it have any vices or bad habits?

Check with vet/buyer
Does the horse have bad habits such as weaving, crib-biting, wind-sucking, rearing, bucking, shying, running away, napping. (Vices must be disclosed.) Has he suffered any recent or recurrent lameness, illness or respiratory problem?

Discuss the horse's past history and ability: has he had any competition successes; is he suitable for your level of ability; is he well-mannered alone and in company? Query any specifics which are important to you: does he ever refuse to jump; will he jump ditches easily? You should try, however, to test these things for yourself, where possible. In some cases an experienced local expert, such as a competition judge or instructor, may be able to vouch for the animal's genuineness.

Trying the horse Try to be the first person that day to see the animal and make sure it has not been previously ridden or turned out. Take an experienced person with you, if possible.

Telephone to warn if you are going to be late or not turn up and don't waste the owner's time if the animal is obviously unsuitable. Note the general standard of the yard and the state of the other horses: do they appear healthy and contented?

Ask to see and handle the horse first in the stable, noting its reactions and demeanour. Note the type of bedding used and if it is soaked.

If the horse is kept permanently at grass, make sure you know the reason – does it dislike being stabled, or become too lively when ridden, or does it have a dust allergy? If you wish to keep it at grass that's fine, but you may need to change its management at some time in the future.

See the horse standing and then walked and trotted up on a hard surface. Look at conformation and for any obvious stiffness, unlevelness or poor action.

If it seems suitable so far, watch it being tacked up and see it ridden, but remember that you need to see how the horse goes for you before it has been worked in for too long. Don't get on a strange horse without first seeing it ridden. Note the type of bit and whether spurs are used (maybe it is headstrong, very sensitive or lazy).

Ideally, ride it first in a confined space and

Another place to look is your local riding school: you may already be interested in a horse there, and know it well, and the owner may wish to keep you as a contented customer. The only drawback is that the horse may have suffered a great deal of wear and tear or may undergo a personality change in less experienced hands or because it is now being worked less hard.

Sales are gaining popularity as a way of gathering together groups of expensive, good-quality horses for viewing and trial that have been proven in competition. Sales at the lower end of the market should be avoided unless you are knowledgeable and are prepared to take a chance regarding soundness, temperament and ability.

Selecting a horse Have ready a list of essential and desirable criteria and don't be deviated from it. Learn to interpret advertisements and vendors' descriptions.

When talking to the vendor, perhaps initially by telephone, have ready a list of pertinent questions and learn to 'read between the lines' without assuming that everyone is dishonest. A vendor may, of course, be reluctant to disclose details which could adversely affect the sale.

If a horse is falsely described you have more chance of legal redress if the statement is in writing or at least made in front of witnesses.

Ask questions which can be answered factually, wherever possible. The vendor's

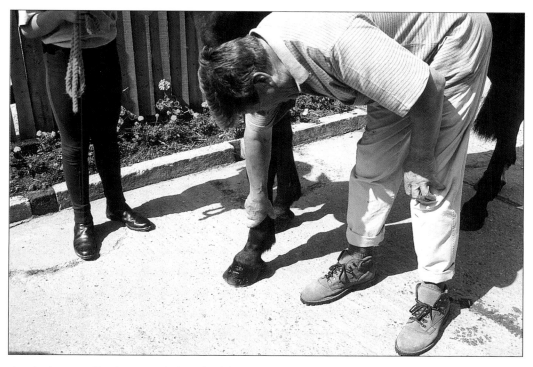

then in the open. Don't overwork the animal but ask to try out or watch the horse's competence in all areas important to you.

Avoid the situation where the horse is set to jump a familiar course or that you take the same course that has already been jumped by the horse with its owner.

If you like the horse, further checks will be:
- Seeing it ridden on the road (preferably the same type of road with volume of traffic you are likely to encounter at home).
- Riding it away from and past its home ground.
- Jumping it over unfamiliar fences.
- Watching it compete, if you are given the opportunity.
- Watching its behaviour at grass and seeing it being caught *(this is more important if you have to share grazing, perhaps at a livery stable)*.

You can learn a lot about a horse's personality by watching how it interacts with other horses. A self-confident but non-aggressive personality is desirable as you will rapidly become unpopular if your horse is aggressive, 'riggy'(behaving like a colt), or is otherwise badly behaved. A timid horse may end up unhappy and isolated, or even injured by unsuitable companions and may be difficult to get in and out of the field safely if other more assertive horses are milling around.

Avoid being pressurized into making a hasty decision. Once you agree to buy (subject to a positive veterinary examination), a cash deposit is usually required and then either cash or some other immediately accessible form of payment when you collect the horse. Make sure you receive a signed and dated receipt and bill of sale which includes a clear description of the horse and that you are given any registration papers, freeze-marking documents, equine influenza and tetanus vaccination documents, etc., at the time.

It is always risky to buy without having a

horse vetted and especially so if it is a valuable animal. Most insurance companies require a vet's certificate before insuring horses over a certain value. Arrange for your own vet or a good local one (not the vendor's) to examine the horse. Be present, if possible, or at least discuss the result with the vet afterwards.

The vet will examine the horse for soundness in all respects. If, at an early stage of his examination, he finds that the horse is lame or ill he will not continue. Otherwise, he will check its height and age and report any lack of absolute soundness of wind and limb as well as abnormalities, including defects of conformation likely to lead to unsoundness. On this basis, and from his overall impression of the horse and its temperament, he will give his opinion as to its suitability for the work you have in mind. If requested, he will take a blood sample which can be tested for drugs should the horse become lame or undergo a dramatic personality change shortly after purchase.

Insure the horse from the moment of purchase and check whether or not vet's fees are immediately covered (many policies exclude this for the first 14 days, when most accidents occur). Arrange for an anti-tetanus vaccination immediately, if this is not already up-to-date.

Find out what the horse has been eating. Purchase a bale of hay and possibly some short feed from the vendor to cover the transitional period and underfeed concentrates initially. Worm the horse and keep it in for at least 24 hrs before turning it out on your pasture.

When the horse arrives at its new home, give it time to settle and familiarize itself with its surroundings. Lead it round the boundaries of its field, if this can be done safely, and introduce it as gradually as possible to new horses to avoid injuries. Ridden work should be sufficient for the horse's level of fitness and nothing stressful or difficult should be asked of it until it has settled in. (It is unfair to take a new purchase to a show the day after it arrives.) Make haste slowly, keeping a watchful eye on the horse's general well-being.

Above left
Your veterinary surgeon should carry out a detailed inspection of the horse before you make a decision to purchase. There are varying degrees of vetting ranging from a simple physical examination to more complicated x-rays and blood tests.

Left
Leading the horse in walk and trot will often reveal unsoundness, but make sure you give the horse plenty of freedom in his head and neck.

Opposite
Always handle a new or strange horse to assess its temperament before riding it.

Chapter Ten
RIDING IN THE MANÈGE

The rider's position: as a guide, look for a vertical line through ear – shoulder – hip – heel, and a straight line from the elbows through the wrist along the reins to the bit. Here the horse is working actively but is a little behind the vertical. He just needs to take a little more weight on the back leg to produce the correct outline.

Before embarking on any kind of training, it is important to develop a good relationship with your horse.

As in a human marriage you need to love each other's virtues while tolerating the faults. Personalities do clash and if you discover you really don't get on with a horse or enjoy its way of going then an amicable divorce may be the best solution.

Life will be much easier if the horse is enthusiastic about its work and is generally relaxed and happy. It is worth asking yourself whether your horse really enjoys the life-style you have chosen for him. Hopefully the answer will be yes! Or maybe a change of emphasis to make life more or less exciting would improve matters.

A sense of humour is an essential attribute. The hours of effort, care and training, not to mention the expense and the millions of things that can go wrong, mean your friends and relations will all be convinced that you are crazy. They have not, however, experienced that special feeling of exhilaration and oneness with a horse when

everything goes magically right.

Be perceptive of your own mood – if you've had a stressful day you may still be wound up and intolerant of the slightest fault. Hacking out or easy, loosening-up work might be preferable. The time to attempt something new and difficult is when you are feeling cheerful and confident. Of course you can't always plan these things to order but if you aren't on top form, go easy on yourself and especially your horse.

Horses often have more sensitivity than we give them credit for – and they usually do go better for someone who really likes them. Although you may be convinced that your riding is the same in competition as it is at home, the horse can sense the difference and will react accordingly.

Develop your horse's trust and confidence in you, and you will gain greater confidence in him. Try to be consistent and fair: discipline is essential and it is no kindness to let your horse take charge. You want to be friends and partners but you must definitely be the one higher up the pecking order. Some horses are so generous that they seem able to guess what you require. Others will quickly learn to take advantage, so you need to correct any small disobedience before it develops into a full-scale rebellion. Some horses will always try their hearts out for you while others (in the minority) will do the bare minimum they can get away with.

If punishment is necessary, it should be rarely administered with the stick and never by yanking on the horse's mouth. Just keeping the horse working should be enough, with a rest or relaxation of the aids as the reward. A word of praise or a pat or scratch on the neck really does encourage the horse: be quick to tell him when he does something right.

Ways to learn

Find a teacher whose approach suits you and who is genuinely keen to see you improve. Have a look at the way they or their pupils ride – is this what you aspire to? Unless you are already experienced, most people find it best to stick to one instructor – different methods can be confusing. Many event riders advocate one trainer for all three disciplines for a consistent approach. Qualifications are a guide to a person's knowledge and ability but results and reputation are just as important. The expensive and fashionable trainer is not necessarily the best choice for a timid novice. For children it is specially important to find someone with whom they can develop a real rapport and have lots of fun. Whoever you choose, make sure they are insured and safety-conscious.

When schooling, get a friend to watch you and comment on your performance: their observations can be very useful. Watch lessons, lecture demonstrations, clinics with top trainers, and good riders working their horses, and begin to formulate a mental picture of your aims and goals.

Remember, the best teachers are horses – ride as many as you can. Listen to them and let them teach you. 'Schoolmasters' (experienced older horses) who know all the tricks will give you confidence and the feel of how things should be done, pointing the way for you to teach and improve your own horse.

At the end of the day, even the best teacher can only facilitate learning. You have to learn in your own time and your own way: one day, in a sudden flash of enlightenment, it may suddenly dawn on you what it is your trainer has been trying to tell you for weeks.

The rider

Riding is all about communicating successfully with your horse. Sitting correctly matters because it enables the rider to stay in balance and give aids easily, unobtrusively and effectively. The basic

Position of the rider

Sitting tall, centralize yourself in the deepest part of the saddle, with your shoulders relaxed back and down, looking ahead. The seat bones should be wide with the legs gently turned to the front from the hips, stretched down and relaxed around the horse's sides without gripping, the heels pressed, but not forced, down. The upper arms should hang relaxed with the elbows gently flexed and the wrists softly rounded. Fingers should be closed with thumbs on top. There should be an imaginary straight line from the elbow through the wrist to the bit, with the hands the width of the bit apart.

A correct position does not develop overnight: it takes time for muscles and joints to loosen, but if you are determined it is achievable. On an everyday basis, stretching and suppling exercises on and off the horse are helpful, and as a warm-up before you ride. It is also useful to have a checklist to run through, concentrating on each part of your body in turn. Run through this often, correcting slight problems before they become major faults.

Staying in balance can be very tiring, especially on a horse with powerful movement so, if you are starting out, a comfortable mover is a much more sensible proposition. Lessons on the lunge are an excellent way to work on your position as you can concentrate entirely on what you are doing without having to think about controlling the horse at the same time. Work without stirrups, either on the lunge or as part of your daily riding practice, will help you to develop a deep, secure seat; but it is important that you don't overdo it at first. As you get tired you will start to grip up, which defeats the whole object of the exercise. You are bound to ache a bit if you have worked hard, but back or joint pain indicates strain or that you are twisting part of your body into an unnatural position and should be investigated.

Although correct posture is important, it is not everything. Given the choice between a rider who looks perfect, but is stiff and fixed, and an untidy rider who doesn't stifle the movement, any horse will prefer the latter. The basis of the position is the seat in the saddle. Always check this first, as problems here will affect the rest of your body.

Symmetry is also important. It is all too easy to lean one way, carry one shoulder higher or further forward than the other or to collapse one hip and sit lopsidedly in the saddle. Other common faults are holding one hand higher or further back than the other and one leg braced forward with the other drawn back and up. Your head is relatively heavy, so tilting it to one side or jutting it forward will affect your balance as well as being a sign of tension. Very often a stiff horse will make a rider sit crookedly: it then becomes a habit and the rider will not only be unable to correct their own horse but may even cause other horses to have similar problems. On the positive side, once you are aware of the problem it just takes persistence to rectify it.

The arm and hand position is designed to enable the rider to maintain an elastic connection with the horse's mouth. It is important to remember to allow your shoulder joints to move, otherwise you will find it difficult to bend your elbows. If you have short upper arms, allow the forearm to relax down a little rather than ending up with your hands held too high, and consequently unsteady: but whatever you do, avoid straight arms with your hands fixed down to the withers and your knuckles facing upwards: it is impossible to maintain a sympathetic contact with the horse's mouth in this position. Riding with too short a rein will produce a similar result, while a too-long rein will tend to make you draw the hands back and stick your elbows out.

principles shown here apply to everyone but it is important to take your own personal conformation into account. Even if we haven't all been born tall, slim and elegant, we can still aim to be balanced and efficient.

The Natural Aids
The rider has a repertoire of aids at his or her disposal. They are rarely if ever used in isolation but combined to produce the desired result. One or more will be active while the others will play a passive, supporting and balancing role. In simple terms, the legs are used to create energy and lateral (sideways) bend and to steer the horse. The reins direct and contain the energy and help with bending, and the back and seat and weight aids connect the two together. One golden rule is that the reins are the *last* link in the chain, never the first. There are many reasons why the horse gives you the 'wrong' reaction or at least one you were not expecting: consider what this might be before apportioning blame. But remember that the one thing you cannot allow is to be totally ignored!

The power of the mind The rider's mental approach is possibly of more importance than all the physical aids put together. Horses tune in instantly to your mood and attitude. They generally respond best to confidence and kindly authority, resenting aggression and ignoring diffidence. Riders tend to fall into two camps – those who always blame the horse and those who always blame themselves. The former attitude is deplorable and ineffective long-term, as a horse will never trust them or try its best for them. The latter, which may contain an element of truth, often leads to the rider never making positive demands of the horse, and can mean that horse and rider never realize their true potential.

The back, seat and weight Perhaps the best advice with regard to using your back and seat is – don't overdo it. Too often, strong 'driving' or 'bracing' aids simply serve to cause the horse to hollow his back. The rider's seat should be 'deep' in the sense that he is supple enough to stay glued to the saddle and go smoothly with the horse's movement. The seat connects and co-ordinates the rider's leg and rein aids but should always allow the horse to move freely 'over the back'. Controlled relaxation from the shoulders down to the seat will allow the rider to adjust the horse's stride by slightly quickening or slowing his own movement, gently lightening his seat or bracing the back *(see Half-halt, page 71)*, or adjusting his weight a little forward or back. Sliding to and fro as though you are polishing the saddle or sitting rigidly still are both to be avoided. Your shoulders should appear still, with no rocking forward or back or twisting. This can only happen if your hips are able to go with the movement. Sometimes thinking of the shoulders moving gently with the horse's back helps to keep them relaxed but steady.

It is important to remember your posture at all times and especially when things are not going smoothly. Tensing and tipping forward, leaning

back, collapsing or hollowing, are all common faults which will affect the horse's response to the rest of your aids and more crucially your balance in times of stress. Surprisingly, however, even slight changes in your weight distribution can sometimes produce very marked changes in your horse's way of going. One often forgotten 'aid' is to look ahead. It is quite possible to steer simply by looking where you want to go – no doubt because, without realizing it, you are making small unconscious weight adjustments. Try this out to see if your other aids are in fact unnecessarily strong.

Above
Riding without stirrups helps develop a deeper, more supple position. This little mare was once almost uncontrollable, but due to her owner's tact and perseverance she is now competing successfully and happily at novice- and elementary-level dressage.

The leg aids The legs can be used in a variety of ways to motivate or steer the horse. The main aim is that the aid should be light and the horse respond instantly to it. Nagging away at the horse's sides at every stride with ever-increasing intensity is unpleasant to watch, wears the rider out, and increasingly numbs the horse's reactions, both mentally and physically. The legs should lightly touch the horse's sides, 'breathing' with the rib cage when not actively employed. They are then ready to give an aid the instant it is needed without startling the horse. A gentle inward press or nudge, repeated as needed, but not constantly, should be enough. If there is no response, try a short sharp nudge or slight kick. If this fails to produce a suitable reaction, check you are not restricting the horse with the rest of your aids. Rather than gradually increasing the aid, give one strong kick to get the horse's attention and make your point. You must be sure that you don't lose your balance or pull back if he jumps forward more sharply than expected. You have said 'go forward', so if you end up going rather faster than you intended, still praise him and slow up gently. Follow this by giving progressively gentler aids, still expecting an immediate response. The whip and spurs are other means of backing up your leg aid and are dealt with in the section on artificial aids *(below)*.

The rein aids The tact and subtlety of the rein aids depend on the rider's ability to go with the movement of the horse (a balanced seat independent of the reins). Hands that move about in sitting trot or canter or go up and down in rising trot (common signs of stiffness or tension) will be unable to keep a smooth elastic connection with the horse's mouth. Relaxed, flexible shoulders, elbows and wrists will allow you to do this. Feel for a light, even, contact through your wrists and elbows. The horse will lean and stiffen against a fixed solid hold but will equally be irritated by an intermittent contact, even if quite light. Repeated small aids are more effective and cause less resistance than one strong one.

When using one rein actively, support and balance the aid by keeping a light contact with the other rein. As well as moderating or assisting the response, this lessens the chance of the horse resisting and the bit pulling partly through his mouth, resulting in discomfort and even more resistance.

With a light contact you can use intermittent increases in pressure with your fingers to ask the horse to relax his jaw and soften his under neck muscles, thus 'giving' to the rider's hand. A quick vibration or shake down the rein can be given if the horse is leaning on the hand. Passively resist if the horse pulls, keeping the hand in place but not allowing it to degenerate into a tug-of-war. Never let yourself get arm-ache. Think what the horse's mouth must feel like! Make a conscious effort to frequently relax your muscles and to work out why this is happening.

The voice Do talk to your horse. It helps you to relax and is a useful back-up to your other aids in soothing, encouraging, or even occasionally, admonishing. Listen to yourself – is that high-pitched, tense voice really yours? Try lowering it an octave. Do you 'click' all the time – this is a sure sign that your horse is not really listening to your legs. Remember, horses have very good hearing so you don't really need to shout!

Use of the voice is penalized in dressage competitions, so keep your voice down and refrain from moving your lips!

The Artificial Aids
The whip This should be used to reinforce the leg aids and only very rarely, if ever, to punish. Be sure you are fair to your horse: if you use the whip to urge him forward, your hands   and body must let him, even if he goes faster than you intended. One clear aid is better than lots   of tentative ones.

A dressage whip can be used with a flick of the wrist while keeping both hands on the reins. However thin, flexible ones can easily mark a sensitive horse.

Put both your reins in the other hand before using a jumping whip or you risk catching the horse in the mouth.

Practise carrying the whip in both hands, changing just after you change the rein (not halfway through – there is too much else to do). If the horse is very one-sided you may want to

The paces

Walk

The sequence of steps is near fore, off hind, off fore, near hind. A good walk is relaxed, moving 'over the back' and should be rhythmic, energetic but unhurried. A correct walk with 4 clear evenly spaced beats is a sign that the training is correct. A **free walk** is an opportunity for the horse to relax and stretch, reaching down and forward with head and neck, stretching over the back so that the top line is round and shoulders free. The nose

should be slightly in front of the vertical as the horse seeks a light contact, the poll level or below the withers. The stride should be long with good over-tracking.

Medium In medium walk, the horse should be on the bit, with medium-length elastic steps and over-tracking.

Transitions When making a transition from medium to free walk, the horse should take the rein down smoothly with no snatching, maintaining rhythm and straightness. Going from a free walk to medium walk the horse should step forward into the rider's hand. The outline should become rounded with no hollowing, the horse maintaining good rhythm and activity. Ride with a generally light leg aid and give a sharp remainder if the horse is lazy rather than nagging at every stride. Keep your back and shoulders gently relaxed, encouraging freedom of movement but never shoving.

In medium walk the hands should go with the horse's head and neck movement without obvious shoving to and fro. When asking for a free walk, keep your hands quietly in place and feed out the rein, allowing the horse to take as much as he wants. Gently playing the reins encourages him to stretch. It is all too easy to ruin a horse's walk by asking for a too restricted outline. If you have problems, stick to a walk on a long rein and get some experienced help.

Left
In medium walk the horse should be on the bit and the steps active with four regular beats to each stride.

Above
Free walk on a long rein. The horse is stretching down well with a rounded top line.

Trot

This is a two-time pace: it should be active, the horse springing from one diagonal pair of feet to the other but flowing smoothly forward and tracking up. In **rising trot**, relax your legs and joints, especially your ankles, as you rise to allow yourself to swing exactly with the movement. If you stiffen, the rise will be too high and jerky or slightly out of time and your hands may move up and down with you.

You can deliberately influence the horse's stride by rising more or less strongly and faster or slower. It is important to rise on the correct diagonal and to spend equal time riding on each diagonal to develop the horse's muscles evenly.

A stiff horse, or one that is lame behind, will try to jolt you off the uncomfortable diagonal.

If you sit when the inside hind-leg is down, it is easier for the horse to carry you and for you to influence him with your leg aids. To start with, you can check which diagonal you are on by looking at the outside shoulder rather than worrying about what the hind-legs are doing. As the outside shoulder (and leg) goes forward and up, so should you. To change the diagonal, sit for two beats. Do this lightly and rise smoothly afterwards so that the horse's rhythm is not disrupted.

In **sitting trot**, it will help you to think of the movement as a wave motion with which your lower back and seat must correspond by moving forward and down each stride. If you still bump, pulling upwards gently on the front of the saddle with one hand will help steady you. Relax your thighs around the horse,

keeping your legs close to the horse's side and your knees soft.

For warming up and with young horses, rising trot is the best choice. Increase the amount of sitting trot gradually as the horse becomes stronger.

Left
Lengthening the strides in trot. The steps are regular but at this angle the horse looks a little on the forehand.

Above
An active working trot. Whenever you and your horse do something really well, memorize that feeling and focus on it whenever you try the exercise again.

moving forward and down with the stride. It is important to sit tall but relaxed. Keep the shoulders steady but be sure that your hands go with the natural forward stretch of the head and neck each stride: it can help to think of moving your hips and hands forward together. Do not be tempted to collapse your back as your legs will draw up and you will tend to come behind the movement and be unable to influence the horse properly. Tipping forward with a tense body is equally problematic. Avoid rocking to and fro: this is exhausting and inefficient and will hollow the horse's back, as will an over-strong driving seat with the rider leaning back. To correct this, some riders find it helps to think of gently pushing the horse's poll forward with your abdomen.

Counter-canter This is deliberately cantering on the 'wrong' lead. It is a suppling and straightening exercise. The horse should continue to bend slightly towards the leading leg, even when he is travelling in the other direction.

It is important that the rider guides the horse by positioning the shoulders and riding from behind rather than pulling the head round. The better his balance, the easier the horse will find it to counter-canter. Common faults are stiffness and tension, loss of rhythm and balance, losing the bend or falling onto the outside shoulder. A good counter-canter will require impulsion. If the horse is on the forehand or has either a too-long or too-quick stride, the exercise will be more difficult. Start by riding very shallow loops and gentle curves not too near the corners until the horse gains confidence and balance.

Above
Working canter. The next moment would show the shoulder being carried more 'uphill'. When warming up and with a young or unmuscled horse, 'sitting light' (shown here) can encourage the horse to relax and stretch his top line.

Canter

This has three beats followed by a period of suspension when all four legs are off the ground. The outside hind-leg starts the stride, followed by the inside hind and outside fore; finally the inside *leading* fore-leg reaches foreward after which there is a moment when the horse is airborne. The pace should be flowing but springy and with a clear period of suspension: a good canter feels like dancing.

A *four-time* canter happens when the diagonal pair of legs stop moving together. It usually means the canter is stiff, tense or laboured. A *disunited* canter is when the horse is, for example, cantering in left lead with the fore-legs and right lead with the hinds. It usually happens as a result of lack of balance on a turn or circle. *Changing leads* behind can also be due to tension or even back trouble. Your lower back should go with the horse's movement,

---

hold it on one side for more but not all the time. Horses learn by association, so if the whip is needed, use it immediately: more than a few second's pause and the horse will not understand why he is being corrected.

Spurs These provide added finesse or reinforce your leg aid, if necessary. They should always be used in addition to, not instead of, your legs. Never kick with spurs.

They should be blunt and straight or angled down, but long enough for you to use without drawing your heels up.

To start with, everyone needs to think about the aids they are giving to improve the overall way of going or for specific movements. It helps to run through the sequence of aids several times in your head or to concentrate on a particular aspect at a time, especially if you are trying to revise something you are doing or learn something new. With practice, your suppleness, co-ordination and 'feel' will develop until you find yourself

reacting almost instinctively, 'programmed' to react with the right aid at the right time.

Lengthening the stride for trot and canter The horse's hind-legs should step under his body with flexible joints 'buoying up' the rider and carrying him forward with a movement which, although it is bigger and more powerful, is still comfortable. Don't entirely blame yourself if you find you cannot sit to your horse's lengthened stride. It could be that he is tensing and hollowing his back, leaving his hocks behind. If this happens, improve the trot, then initially try just a few strides sitting at a time.

The rhythm should stay exactly the same. The most common fault is for the horse to quicken rather than lengthen. The ability to lengthen on request develops as the horse learns to engage his hocks and work with controlled energy. To start with, a stronger leg aid (smoothly with the rhythm of the stride and not a kick) and a more obvious swing of your body in rising trot, or a forward feel

with your seat, will give encouragement. Eventually, the horse will lengthen enthusiastically as you release the contained energy, allowing him to lengthen his frame. The horse should step from the leg into the hand which then allows for lengthening. If you give too soon or too much he will probably run onto his forehand or hollow rather than stepping under from behind.

Try to relax your shoulders and go with the horse with your lower back, rather than gripping up – it also helps to breathe!

The correct way of going

The horse will look happy and relaxed but attentive. His movement will look and feel more expressive and elastic and although more powerful, will feel smooth. He will look more beautiful as the correct muscles develop and work.

He should be calm, confident and alert, obedient and quick to react and moving actively forward with regular rhythmic steps into a soft, even contact with the rider's hands. He should be supple throughout his body, enabling the energy from the hind-legs to work through over his back to the bit, and so to the rider's hands, creating a rounded outline, his face just in front of the vertical. He should feel 'uphill' with the hind-legs carrying more of the weight than they would in nature, lightening the forehand and increasing manoeuvrability.

As the horse's training progresses, his muscles will develop, his strength and suppleness increase, and he will be able to carry more and more weight on the hind-legs, leading to increased collection and better self-carriage. You are now experiencing that lovely feeling when the horse can dance through the movements in perfect balance without the need to lean on your hands for support.

So how are we to produce such a paragon? First of all, although good conformation and paces obviously help, you do not need an extravagantly moving warm-blood. Don't assume your ordinary sort of horse can only ever be average. Watch him moving loose in the field when something has excited him – there is no reason why he can't move like that under the saddle: but he won't unless you ask him to. It is often easier to start from scratch with a young horse than to improve an older one set in its ways; but old horses can learn new tricks even though old joints and

muscles take longer to loosen and supple.

First of all, try to tune in to the horse and work it in a way that minimizes stress on all concerned. It isn't always possible to avoid all tension and resistance but that should certainly be your aim. It is particularly important to remember that tension and apparent naughtiness may well be due to the horse finding the work physically difficult or confusing. A change for the better in the horse's temperament is a good sign that the training is correct. It is amazing the extent to which a neurotic, agitated animal can calm down or a lazy, inattentive one become motivated and energetic with the correct type of work.

Right from the word go, you should instil the basics. There is no point allowing the horse to work in a stiff unbalanced manner for months, then suddenly deciding to teach it a better way. This also applies to your daily riding. Hacking out should be relaxing and fun but the horse can still be ridden correctly so that he develops the right muscles and stays balanced and attentive.

It is important to match the difficulty of the movements to the level of training. A young horse may be able to manage large circles and progressive transitions smoothly and confidently, but struggle to cope with small circles or direct transitions and end up tensing, losing his rhythm

and becoming anxious and resistant.

The rider's skill is to recognize when to ask a more difficult question and how quickly to progress. For this, you need knowledge, understanding and observation.

Let the horse tell you how well he is coping, whether he is bored or overwhelmed. Horses react to stress in different ways. Some become obviously tense, others mentally shrink into themselves and may appear lazy and unco-operative. Keeping the horse's interest is important. If you are too cautious, the horse can switch off both mentally and physically. Vary the school movements rather than getting stuck on the outside track of a 20-metre (66-ft) circle. Changes in direction and more complicated shapes will reveal stiffness, lack of balance or poor reaction to the aids, but if not overdone will also often motivate the horse to make a little more effort to help himself and emphasize to the rider where improvements are needed. It is all too easy to subconsciously stick to things you know you can do well and avoid problem areas. This is one value of competition work – it focuses your mind on particular movements that you might otherwise 'forget' to practise.

The training should follow a logical progression, but there will obviously be a lot of

---

Some common training terms explained

- **Collected, working, medium and extended**
  Terms referring to the length of the horse's frame and stride and amount of weight it is carrying with its hindquarters.
- **Tempo** The speed/rate of the strides.
- **Rhythm** The evenness and regularity of the strides. Each horse has its own natural rhythm.
- **Outline** The shape and carriage of the horse's head, neck. That is, rounded or hollow, novice or advanced.
- **Activity** Energy combined with freedom of movement: the raw material of impulsion.
- **Impulsion** This is controlled energy, when the hind-legs step actively forward under the horse's body and the forward power is gently contained and directed by the rider's hands: the result is an elastic, springy stride and a feeling of controlled power.

  When told that your horse 'lacks impulsion' it is tempting to push it on faster. Speed is not the same thing at all and will only result in a flat-running stride with loss of balance and tension.
- **On the forehand** This means that too great a proportion of the horse's weight is being carried by the front legs. The horse feels as though it is travelling 'downhill' and will often lean on the rider's hands.
- **Balance** Good balance is relative to the stage of training. It means that the weight

distribution over the horse's limbs enables it to describe the shapes required, easily maintaining an even rhythm and tempo.
- **Engagement** When the horse responds to the rider's aids by stepping further under its body, flexing its joints and lowering the hind-legs, consequently carrying more of the weight on the hindquarters.
- **Half-halt** A moment to check and re-balance the pace and gain the horse's attention at any time, but particularly before transitions to other paces or more difficult movements.

  The rider closes the lower leg around the horse, lightly 'braces' the back (stretches and firms the lower back) pausing with the seat and then almost simultaneously applies a light rein aid. In this way, the rider is creating a little more energy with the legs while the seat and reins say 'no faster'. As a result, the horse should shift its weight a little more onto its hind-legs, stepping forward with improved balance and lightness and attention. This should all take only about a second and be barely noticeable but can be repeated frequently. Occasionally, a stronger reminder may be needed.

  A useful schooling exercise to improve the horse's reactions and suppleness is a more obvious version where the rider makes a downward transition from trot to walk, then asks the horse to trot on again after only two to three steps. The horse should stay rounded and 'working through' and respond immediately to the aids.

- **Resistance** Objection to the rider's requests. This could manifest itself as ears laid back, swishing tail or grinding teeth, through to hollowing and fighting the rein aids, leaning into or kicking against the leg aid, napping or running back, rearing or bucking. This can be caused by physical discomfort, mental anxiety or loss of confidence or inability to do what is asked. Or it could be caused by the rider's poor balance/suppleness/aids or due to bad manners on the part of the horse – unused to discipline and outside influences (inattention, excitement).

Always remember that horses are animals, even though we tend to endow them with all kinds of human attributes. We forget that they do not have our intelligence or reasoning powers and expect them to concentrate for longer than we can and to react instantly to the aids we mean to give, while ignoring our accidental kicks and tugs. We punish over-enthusiasm and slow reactions in equal measure and expect them to stay in perfect balance when we can't even keep our own heels down.

Horses may not be over-bright but they are incredibly generous, very sensitive, and have phenomenal memories. It takes a very long time for a horse to forget a good or bad experience.

Remember that success or failure short-term is less important than making progressive improvement over a space of time.

overlapping and horses are so individual that much flexibility is needed.

To start with, the horse must respect the rider's aids to go forward and to stop and turn in their simplest forms. Correct regular paces and even rhythm and tempo are your next concern.

Contact This is the connection down the reins between the rider's hands and the horse's mouth. The horse should be encouraged to accept an elastic contact with the rider's hands, relaxing his jaw and at the poll. He should seek out the contact, reaching forward to *take the rider by the hand*, rather than the rider pulling back. The strength of the contact will vary from horse to horse and depend on the level of schooling and self-carriage and exactly what is being asked of the horse. Ultimately, the horse should take as even as possible a contact on both reins without tension and resistance. A novice working correctly from inside leg and outside hand should have a slightly lighter contact in the inner rein when circling and turning. Common faults are intermittent contact caused by inactivity, stiffness, or the rider having unsteady hands or an uneven pull on one or both reins, the horse setting his jaw against the rider's hand. The horse can also 'drop' the contact which means that he draws his nose back to evade the rider's hands.

Suppling This will improve the horse's ability to bend laterally (sideways) and longitudinally (from tail to poll) and to negotiate circles and turns in balance. This is made much easier if the horse listens to the leg and responds to the aids calmly. There may be times when, in trying to make improvements, you seem to be taking a step backwards. For example, when asked to bend laterally with the inside leg, the horse may well just rush forward against the rider's hand, losing

Top
This young ex-racehorse, during her first lesson in the arena, is not yet seeking out a contact with the rider's hands and is very hollow in her outline.

Above centre
The same horse a few weeks later is already working in a much rounder outline and with lots of activity.

Above
Her canter is very 'on the forehand'. As her muscles develop this will improve. Her head and neck shape means that it is easy for her to work 'deep', coming behind the vertical. The rider will have to take care not to encourage this.

Left
Straightness is most important and horse and rider often influence one another. The horse is moving quarters-in on the left rein. The rider and saddle have slipped to the outside, making the situation worse.

his rhythm. In cases like this you have to decide whether this is a temporary setback until the horse understands what is required of him, or whether he just isn't ready for this stage.

All horses are more able to bend one way than the other. As the suppling work progresses this should even out until the horse takes as nearly as possible an even contact on both reins and responds equally to both legs.

Straightness The horse should be straight throughout his body when moving on a straight line and evenly bent to conform to the curve when on a circle.

Straightness and suppleness are interconnected. In making the horse able to bend equally both ways you are in effect straightening him. Also, if a horse is stiff through his back he will try to shift his quarters to one side to avoid the effort of stepping under the body with the hind-legs and so will be crooked. (This is very common in canter, the horse going quarters-in.)

Lateral bend Between the withers and the croup the horse can bend his spine sideways only a tiny amount (in the lumber region). Suppling work concentrates on teaching the muscles to extend and contract more efficiently, freeing up the joints. The result is a horse who looks and feels as though he is bending throughout his body, his hind-legs following the track of the fore-legs.

The shoulders should feel level and upright and the withers should be central between them. (Look and see if there is equal bulk either side.) On a circle or turn, the head and neck must bend only as much as the rest of the body (usually just allowing you to see the inside eyelashes). On the straight, the horse's spine should be parallel to the track. The horse is shaped like a triangle (quarters wider than withers) so if you line the outside of his body up to the outer wall he will be going quarters-in.

The neck is so flexible that it is quite easy for the horse to bend it without his body following. This can equal lack of control! It is important to think of positioning the shoulders rather than the head.

Longitudinal bend A powerful ligament attaches like an elastic cable from the top of the skull along the neck to the withers where it joins another ligament which extends along the back to the point of the croup. When the horse's head and neck stretch forward and down, these ligaments tighten, pulling the back up and making it easier for the horse to step under his body from behind, and to carry the rider's weight. The nuchal (neck) ligament also supports the head and neck, allowing the muscles to raise and lower it. Pulling backwards with the reins causes the ligaments to slacken, the back to hollow and the hind-legs to trail out behind. Correct training will strengthen the ligaments and muscles helping the horse to move correctly.

For this reason, in the early stages of training the outline should be long and low. When the horse is moving correctly, the back and withers lift, buoying up the rider and allowing a freer stride, the horse pressing the crest forward to the poll and seeking out a contact with the rider's hands. As the horse becomes stronger, he will be able to step further under and carry more weight with the hind-legs working in a shorter frame with the head and neck carried higher.

Forcing the head and neck into position will result in the base of the neck dropping and the back lowering which will produce discomfort, fatigue and poor muscle development. Unfortunately, it is quite possible for the horse to be very hollow through his body despite his neck being arched and his head held in.

As you can see, working to develop lateral bend and straightness will also develop suppleness from tail to poll. Transitions *(pages 74–75)* between and within the paces and half-halts will further increase the horse's suppleness and strength.

By this time, the next stage, the horse working in a rounded outline 'to the bit' *(page 75)*, will be well on the way to developing naturally. As the horse becomes supple throughout his body he will learn to work from the leg and seat up to the bit and to accept a soft contact with the rider's hand (relaxing his jaw and at the poll).

Circles and turns Remember that a turn is just a segment of a small circle. Check your speed, rhythm and stride length; you can't negotiate circles and turns in balance if your stride is too long or too fast.

Start by looking where you want to go and, turning your upper body gently in the direction of the circle, keep your shoulders parallel to the horse's. When riding a stiff horse it is very easy to end up with your inside shoulder leading – this makes you far less effective. Sit centrally and absolutely straight with a little more weight to the inside. Check that you do not end up sitting to the outside of the saddle. It is important that the rider's inside leg remains on the girth, asking the horse to step forward and under the body with the inside hind-leg enabling the rider to receive the energy in the outside rein which is held quite close to the neck, controlling the speed and guiding the horse round the circle.

The outside leg should be placed behind the girth, controlling the quarters and stopping them from swinging out and helping with the forward movement.

The inside rein is the last link. It helps to position the horse's shoulders round the circle and asks the horse to relax his jaw and flex softly to the inside. Think of your reins as creating a tunnel through which to channel the horse with your legs and try never to pull back with the inside rein.

Usually, the hands will be positioned the normal width apart and slightly to the inside. However, a more open inside rein is helpful to encourage a young horse in the correct direction. Resist the impulse to fix the inside hand into the neck or draw the outer hand away to keep the horse out on the circle, and never ever pull one hand across to the other side of the withers.

All horses are stiffer one way than the other.

When circling or turning, the horse should feel upright in his shoulders. Here, the horse is over-turning his neck and 'falling out' through the outside shoulder. The rider is pulling back with the inside rein, making matters worse and causing the bit to slide through the horse's mouth.

When circling on their stiff rein they will 'fall in', carrying too much weight on the inside shoulder, leaning on the inside rein and finding it difficult to bend to the inside.

On the softer side they may 'fall out', overbending the neck to the inside and drifting out with excess weight on the outer shoulder. At other times they will ignore the inside leg and cut in on the circle, pulling away from the restraint of the outside rein. If they are nappy or inattentive they will find it easy to use their lack of suppleness to evade your control.

The answer is to improve the suppleness and correct the position of the shoulders as far as possible with the leg aids. This in itself will help even up the feeling in the hands. It may be helpful to do a little more work on the horse's stiff rein to 'even him up' but be careful not to overdo it, causing fatigue and more resistance. Switching to the easier rein and then back again can work wonders.

It can be helpful at times to exaggerate the inside bend in the neck or flex the horse to the outside to loosen and soften it, but you must remember to straighten again afterwards.

The horse must respond to the inside leg and step into a contact with the outside rein before you ask for bend and softening with the inner rein, otherwise he will either resist, bend too much or turn in. Keep the pace calm and slow until the horse learns to bend rather than quicken. On the horse's soft side, keep the inner hand very quiet, maintaining a light steady contact while the outer rein 'asks' the horse not to lean or fall out, helped by the outer leg which is moved forward to the girth if necessary. Try not to fix the hand or be too strong or the horse will lean on you more.

If you don't seem to be having much success with a stiff horse, go back to walk or even halt. Start by gently asking the horse to 'give' to the inner rein and flex his head and neck right round to the inside. Relax the inner rein as he does so. The outer rein maintains a light contact but allows the horse to take its head and neck round to the inside.

Repeat the exercise on a circle in walk, using a clear inside leg. As the horse starts to react and step out into a contact with the outside rein, reduce the bend. You can then try spiralling in to reduce the circle size then leg yield back out. Work to improve the horse's response to the leg, lightening the rein and gradually progressing to 20-m (65-ft) circles in trot.

Bending the horse around your inside leg Once the horse is responding to your inside leg, rather than thinking of pushing the horse out, think of bringing the shoulders in front of your inside leg to create the bend. When changing direction, allow enough time to adjust the horse's body from one bend through at least a moment of straightness before asking for the other bend.

Left
When circling, the outside leg should be positioned a little behind the girth, keeping the quarters from swinging out.

Below
A canter transition with horse and rider in good balance. At this moment the horse is slightly above the bit but is showing little resistance. The rider's reins are a little too long.

Corners Make sure you prepare the horse for the corner and straighten him as he comes out of it. Sometimes you will need to adjust your aids to counteract what the horse is doing. For example: on the horse's stiff rein, if he tries to cut the corner, try steadying the pace to enable you to increase the inner leg as you approach the corner, thinking of riding straight through the fence, your seat bones pressing straight forward. Once he starts to listen, you can begin to ask him to bend. On the 'softer' rein he may over-turn the neck to the inside; you then need to half-halt on the outer rein as you approach the corner: use minimal inner rein and a quiet inside leg and then just soften the outer rein as you turn. Remember to straighten the horse again as you start to come out of the corner, otherwise you may end up with him going down the long side banana-shaped or even trying to turn across the diagonal.

When a stiff horse ignores your leg aid, it is tempting to use too much rein. This can lead to the horse tilting its head to one side so that one ear is higher than the other. A head tilt is generally an indication that the horse is finding it a struggle to bend correctly but it can sometimes be due to muscle spasm in the neck, slight misalignment of the vertebrae, or mouth problems.

Upward transitions Apply the legs lightly but clearly (on the girth), the seat and lower back pressing gently forward with the movement (don't shove or hollow your back). The hands maintain the same contact, but allow the movement. If you get a lazy response, activate the lower pace next time, then use a light aid; if this doesn't work give a sharp aid, backed up with the whip, if necessary, and allow as much forwardness as is offered. Repeat the exercise, but this time much more gently. If the outline hollows it indicates that the horse is not working 'over' his back; he may be tense and not accepting the leg. This could be because the rider's hands are too fixed or the seat

is too strong or you have given a clumsy leg aid.

When first learning to go in a rounder outline, the horse may hesitate and feel unable to work out how to make the transition without his usual lift of the head; allow him a stride or two to sort himself out, it will improve with practice.

Start with progressive transitions, e.g. halt–walk–trot, gradually reducing the number of strides in the intervening pace until the horse can cope with direct transitions such as halt-trot. Use a clear aid with a deep seat but take care not to stiffen. Direct upward transitions are easier than direct downward ones.

Canter transitions To help the balance and encourage the correct lead, ask for the transition to canter when approaching a corner or on a 20-m (65-ft) circle as you approach the track.

Later, teach the horse to respond to the aid wherever you ask – do take care to balance and prepare him first and keep a slight bend around the inside leg. Ride at least a few strides of sitting trot, checking you are sitting square in the saddle, and keep the inside leg deep and close to the horse at the girth. Draw the outside leg back a hand's breadth (quietly), then immediately close both legs with a press or nudge. The inner seat bone should be pressing a little forward and down as you do so. Sit up straight and try not to tip forward or back. The rider should have an elastic contact on the outer rein, the inner rein and leg asking for the bend. Soften the inner hand a little on strike-off to allow freedom of the movement.

If the horse strikes off on the wrong leg it may be because the rider is crooked and out of balance, or giving an incorrect aid, or is asking too late when the horse is coming out of the corner, or that the horse is stiff, tense or unbalanced.

The most important thing is to persuade the

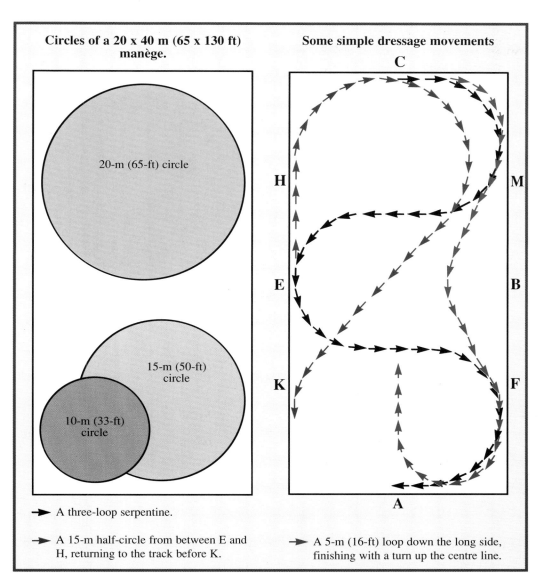

Circles of a 20 x 40 m (65 x 130 ft) manège.

20-m (65-ft) circle

15-m (50-ft) circle

10-m (33-ft) circle

→ A three-loop serpentine.

→ A 15-m half-circle from between E and H, returning to the track before K.

Some simple dressage movements

→ A 5-m (16-ft) loop down the long side, finishing with a turn up the centre line.

Once the horse is stepping forward into a contact you can, if necessary, 'ask' softly on the heavier rein for the horse to 'give' and relax his jaw while the other hand maintains a steady contact. Feel the exact type of squeeze or 'give and take' with your fingers that suits your horse. *Softer* often works better than *stronger* – intermittant jerks and heavy pulls are out! If in doubt, soften sooner rather than later as this encourages the horse to relax and you can always repeat the aid if you misjudged the moment. Asking the horse to go on the bit on a circle is usually more effective than in a straight line. As the horse starts to respond, relax the aid and hold the contact softly and steadily, rewarding the horse and showing him that he has done the right thing. He may well try to stretch more forward and down – this is fine at the start. Go with him, only correcting him if he tries to stick his nose out and snatch at the rein.

Should the horse try to 'drop' the contact, going 'behind the bit', press him forward firmly with your legs and try to feel for a quiet connection with his mouth, even if he draws his head back behind the vertical (over-bent). You can then encourage him to take your hands forward again as he starts to move into the contact. He may be over-reacting to clumsy rein aids or a too severe bit, or have the sort of head/neck set that makes it easy for him to flex his head without working 'through' from behind.

A firmer aid for a few seconds is preferable to nagging away without any real result. Equally, releasing the contact on the stiffer side completely for a couple of seconds as the horse gives, will offer him a big 'thank you' but the 're-take' to a soft contact must be smooth

Be careful you don't end up with a rhythmical tug/release – the horse bracing himself against the pull and just waiting for you to give. Constant fiddling away at the horse's mouth is equally bad.

Another fault which can be difficult to cure is the horse swinging his nose left/right in response to the rider's rein aids.

If the horse leans or resists strongly you probably haven't done your groundwork properly.

One common fault is for the rider to allow the horse to lift his head, lightening the contact as he does so, but to hang on for grim death when he does offer a rounder outline in the hope of keeping his head in place. This is obviously sending entirely the wrong signals to the horse, and punishing him whenever he tries to do the right thing. Riders usually do this completely subconsciously. You should never try to hold or pull the horse's head into position. Press him forward into a contact if he raises his head and, as he stretches forward and down into the hand, you can then ask him to soften again.

It is important to match the length and carriage of the horse's neck with the rest of his body. In theory, with correct riding this will happen automatically, but in practice it is quite easy to end up with the neck too short or high. This will lead to resistance or a restricted stride. If in doubt, think of maintaining the balance through the horse's body as you lengthen the neck and do so a bit more than you think you should.

inside hind to step actively forward under the horse's body. Be careful he does not turn his neck too much to the inside and fall out with the shoulder or lean in with the wrong bend.

Downward transitions Prepare the horse by using half-halts; this will bring him more onto his hind-legs and therefore achieve better balance. Smaller aids repeated several times are better than one strong one. Sit deeply into the saddle, lowering the knee and heel softly with a feeling of 'pausing' as you slightly brace your back, close the legs, and quietly ride forward into a lightly resisting hand. Close the fingers and gently flex the elbows, relaxing your shoulders. Think 'hips to hands'. If there is no immediate response, feel or play the rein rather then fix the hands. Don't forget to relax the leg aid as the horse responds or he will become confused! Check that you don't almost stop riding just before the transition as you concentrate – and remember to ride the first few strides afterwards fluently forward.

Timing the aids Good timing of the aids will make it easier for the horse to respond smoothly. This is especially apparent in transitions. It takes

practice to feel the right moment (in the stride) to give the aid when the horse's balance is just right. For most people, relaxing and letting it all happen subconsciously works far better than thinking about it – a good instructor will be able to guide you. Generally speaking, keeping with the rhythm of the pace works best (even when using the whip) to produce a smooth reaction without disrupting the horse's concentration. Quickening the leg aid will produce a sharper reaction.

Riding the horse on (or to) the bit If you supple the horse as described, working 'on the bit' is a comfortable and natural progression. The phrase refers to the whole horse working from behind, up to the rider's hand and adopting a rounded outline (*see The correct way of going, page 70*). A horse with reasonable conformation will be able to relax at the poll and jaw as he presses forward to the rider's hands, carrying his face just in front of the vertical. Horses with thick or 'ewe necks', or poor conformation, will find this more difficult. The longer and lower the outline at first, the easier it will be for them to soften and flex. A horse that has learned bad habits will also take longer to learn to respond correctly.

walk, with active steps. The inside fore-leg must
not swivel or get 'stuck'. A full turn is 180°, a half
turn is 90°.

How to ride it When teaching this, ask for one
step at a time, gradually building up to the full
turn. First teach the horse to move over in hand.
Under saddle, positioning the horse facing the wall
may help him understand what is required initially.
Allow room for a full turn by starting along the
inner track or choose an open space with a
sluggish horse. The rider's inside leg (left for a left
turn) slightly behind the girth asks the hind legs to
move away and cross step by step. The rider's
outer leg stays close to the horse's side, ready to
encourage him forward if he tries to 'stick' or step
back, and to straighten him if he tries to shift his
weight onto his outside shoulder and shuffle
sideways rather than turning. The rider sits tall and
straight, the hands working together to contain the
movement, to prevent the horse from walking
forward and to keep the shoulders straight. The
inner hand asks for a slight flexion to the inside,
taking great care not to pull the head round. The
outer rein can help to balance the horse, with light
half-halts as he turns. It is important to think
forward all the time and avoid pulling back. Once
the movement is completed, ride forward briskly.
If he ignores your aids and walks head first up to
the wall, don't drag him round with the reins
while still asking the hind-legs to cross; tactfully
turn and walk him forward.

Leg yield The horse moves forward and sideways,
his body and neck straight with slight flexion at
the poll away from the direction of the movement.
He must travel at least as much forward as
sideways and to start with somewhat more.

He should keep his rhythm, swinging through
his back and moving with active, elastic steps. Leg
yield is usually performed in walk and trot but it
can be ridden in canter. Once the horse is familiar
with the movement it is a useful loosening
exercise. Common faults are leading with the
shoulders, the quarters trailing, and leading with
the quarters which is much more serious as the
horse cannot move forward freely.

An easy starting place is from the quarter-line
back to the track, as the horse will be keener to
move back to 'home ground'. Once he is familiar
with the aids, he can be asked to move away from
the track; this puts more onus on the response to
the leg aid. Leg yield on the circle can help to
supple the horse. The fore- and hind-legs should
cross evenly, the horse maintaining inside bend as
the circle size increases.

Leg yield can be ridden along the track at an
angle, with the quarters to the wall. The
drawbacks are that it is harder to set it up
smoothly and maintain the forward momentum
and it can cause confusion later with shoulder-in,

Lateral Work
Leg yield and turn on (or about) the forehand
These are the simplest lateral movements and can
be taught to the horse at quite an early stage in
his training. They teach increased response to the
aids, help to supple and loosen the horse, and
increase his manoeuvrability. In addition, they
provide the rider with useful practice in co-
ordinating the aids.

At first, there can seem to be far too many
things to think about and to do at once; a common
fault is the rider stiffening and forgetting to go
with the horse's movement because they are
concentrating so hard.

Before you attempt the movement, check that
you understand exactly what the horse is supposed
to be doing, that you are clear as to the aids

required and know how to correct any obvious
faults. To start with, you will be doing well if you
manage to recognize how the horse is responding,
let alone correct mistakes as you go along. With
practice, your arms and legs will start to function
separately as and when needed and everything will
fall into place.

Turn on the forehand This can be ridden from
the halt (turn *on*) or after a half-halt from a
balanced walk (turn *about*), which helps maintain
the essential forward movement. The horse turns
his quarters around his forehand, crossing his
hind-legs, his body straight with a slight flexion at
the poll away from the direction in which the legs
are moving, i.e., left in a left turn. All four legs
must keep moving in the correct sequence for the

encouraging the horse to swing his quarters out.

The inside leg (right if the horse is travelling to the left) either on or just behind the girth (to make the aid cleaner) asks the horse to move over (press for each step, quick nudges if the reaction is slow). The outside leg helps keep the forward impulse and controls the shoulder. The inside hand asks for slight flexion and assists the outside hand in guiding the shoulders sideways. The outside hand also controls the speed forward and across and the position of the outside shoulder, straightening the horse with the help of the outside leg. The rider should sit tall and central, shoulders square to the horse's, a little more weight in the inside leg, looking ahead or in the direction of the movement. Initially the hands may need to 'lead' the shoulders in the sideways direction until the horse gets the idea. Then they should stay central or positioned a little away from the direction of movement if the horse is tending to lead too much with the shoulders.

Shoulder-in

This is an important suppling exercise and helps to teach the horse to carry more weight on his hind-legs.

The horse should be working consistently to the bit and understand the basic aids to move sideways before you start to teach this. It is a strenuous movement, so start with a few steps at a time. The usual place to teach it is along the track, though once the horse is confident it can be ridden anywhere.

The horse moves sideways on three tracks, bent throughout his body evenly, away from the direction of the movement, his inside hind-leg following the track of the outside fore. The rider

sits centrally, shoulders parallel to the horse's, with rather more weight on the inside seat bone. The inside leg acts at the girth to ask the horse's inside hind-leg to step under his body. The outside leg, a little behind the girth, controls the position of the quarters which must not swing out, but also helps place the shoulders more to the inside, if

necessary. Both hands are carried a little to the inside of centre, the outer one controlling the angle and position of the shoulders and the speed, the inner hand very lightly leading the forehand in and asking for just enough bend. The horse should keep his rhythm and forewardness (he may well hesitate when first learning) and not over-bend his neck or stiffen and resist. Common rider faults which will contribute to this are to sit crooked, draw the inner heel back, or drag the inner rein against the neck.

Rein-back

Only when the horse works in a rounded outline and accepts the halt aids without resistance should you begin to teach this. You can show the horse what you want, in hand to start with, using your voice and a push with your hand or a gentle tap on the legs with a whip. Your voice is then an added help when you are mounted. Ask for one or two steps initially, and not too often, as it is very strenuous. Make sure to reward the horse. If he resists, a helper on the ground is useful. Don't ask if the horse is hollow with his head up as it is then physically very difficult.

Start from an alert halt with the horse in a fairly low and round outline; close the legs (a little behind the girth) and slightly lighten your seat. As the horse goes to step forward, the hand re-directs the energy backwards. Don't let yourself pull back. Facing the horse to the wall may initially help him understand. Positioning him along the wall will help keep him straight. The horse should clearly move his legs back in diagonal pairs without dragging his feet. He must stay calm and balanced and not rush back. Too large a step initially may make him lose some balance and the correct diagonal steps.

The Schooling Session

Riders often complain that they don't know what to do when they are working on their own, that they get bored and wander around aimlessly. Here are some guidelines and suggestions to help you plan your training.

As a rule, 45 minute's actual work suits most horses and 20–30 minutes is ample for the young or unfit (horse or rider!). If the horse gives you some exceptional work, by all means give him a hug and stop there or maybe go for a hack or turn him out instead.

Make sure you always give the horse (and yourself) ample time to warm up. If you are short of time, stick to simple loosening work; don't be tempted to practise difficult movements before you are both warmed up, allowing insufficient time to sort out inevitable problems.

Progressively build up to more difficult work but avoid leaving it too late in the session when the horse is beginning to tire mentally and physically. If you feel the work is deteriorating, have a walk on a long rein and try to work out why. Repeating an exercise over and over again isn't always the answer, especially if you keep on making the same mistake! You don't want

yourself or your horse to get hung up over a particular exercise. It helps to have a focus – it might be improving the bend and suppleness, getting more activity or working on the straightness.

Try focusing on accuracy, using the markers if it helps. Practise a variety of school movements and concentrate on the correct way of going. Remember to work on transitions and use one pace to enliven or calm another. Try not to get stuck in one pace for too long.

Use lateral work in short spells with forward thinking or calming work in between, depending on the horse's personality. Try lengthening and shortening the stride to keep the horse listening and improve his agility and balance.

Keep an eye on your position and have several breaks in walk on a long rein for you both to relax and stretch.

Always finish on a good note with some easy work that the horse does well and that you both enjoy, ending up with the horse stretching down with a long but rounded outline. Walk on a loose rein for a few minutes before you take him in.

Chapter Eleven
LUNGEING

Lungeing is a useful way of exercising a horse which, for whatever reason, cannot be ridden. It can also settle an over-fresh horse before riding it. It helps to develop communication, confidence, and a sense of calm leading to obedience and attention, and can be used as the basis for the schooling of the young horse. It develops suppleness, balance and dexterity, improving muscular development and fitness. It also teaches the horse regularity, rhythm, and activity of the paces.

Lungeing is a valuable exercise, both for horse and rider. Unfortunately, it can also be extremely detrimental if done badly. Working constantly on a circle is strenuous and it is all too easy to cause strains or damage a horse's joints. Young, unbalanced and unfit horses, in particular, are quite likely to brush or knock their legs, especially if they are fresh and playful. As a result, some people feel it is unwise to lunge horses coming into work. Certainly, if your horse is calm enough to let you ride it sensibly from the start of its fitness programme you can leave lungeing until it is coping well with undemanding schoolwork, in trot.

The situation is rather different with unbacked youngsters. Here lungeing is a valuable training aid, developing the horse's confidence and rapport with you and teaching him to respond to the voice, rein and whip, both to go forward and stop. From this simple start, work on the lunge will develop the young horse's muscles and begin to supple and strengthen him. He will start to bend correctly on the circle and with the use of side reins learn to accept and relax to a light contact with his mouth. All of this will make the process of backing him and riding away easier and less traumatic for both horse and rider.

If the work is undertaken carefully and progressively by an experienced person, then all should be well. Problems generally arise only if the trainer is either inexperienced or unobservant. Horses are very quick to learn both good and bad habits. For every generous soul who will give you the benefit of the doubt there will be a stronger personality who will learn fast that he can get the upper hand. A horse that simply lacks confidence in you may also start to misbehave or even panic. It is important to start gently and build up the work gradually to avoid stresses and strains. Overworking the horse both in terms of individual sessions and over a period of time can easily make him sour and unwilling, either because he is physically sore or tired or from boredom and dislike of the work. This may well colour his attitude to subsequent ridden work.

So how do you avoid the pitfalls? Lungeing is one of those skills that looks a lot easier than it is. Do not despair! Start practising with a calm horse

This four-year-old Lusitano mare is tacked up ready to be lunged in a snaffle bridle and lungeing cavesson with side reins. Ideally, the noseband would be a little higher but this was the best adjustment for her head shape. Unclip the side reins if standing still for more than a moment.

who knows his job; an experienced teacher to demonstrate and then guide you is a huge help. At first you may well feel unco-ordinated and rather inept, but do persevere.

For the horse to benefit from lungeing he must first be taught calmness and obedience, respecting the voice aids, the restraint of the lunge rein, and the forward-driving aids of the whip with confidence and without fear.

He must learn to work actively forward in a good rhythm with regular paces and on a true circle. He should also be encouraged to move away from the whip, taking a steady but light contact on the lunge rein and to bend in the direction of the circle. His hind-legs should follow in the track of the fore-legs and he should not fall in or out with his shoulders. Check that his back is relaxed and swinging and that he is 'tracking up'.

Don't underestimate the importance of body language. At all times be quiet and confident and give clear, positive aids, closely observing the

horse's reactions. His expression will often warn you of his intentions!

The position of the handler relative to the horse is all-important. If you are too far forward (getting 'in front' of the horse) you will have difficulty sending the horse forward and may even encourage him to turn in. If too far back, you will have problems developing correct bend and a true circle and will also have little control over excess forward movement. The handler should face towards the horse, slightly turned in the direction of movement. Always try to avoid the need to step backwards.

Ideally the handler should stay still, pivoting in the centre of the circle. This, however, is often impractical for control and effectiveness. It is acceptable to shorten the rein, moving closer to the horse, and walking a small circle without wandering.

Your whip should always be held low (you are not a lion tamer!). Generally, it should point towards the horse's hip but you can move it a little further back to drive the horse forward or towards the girth, or even shoulder, to discourage the horse from 'falling in' on the circle. (Watch you don't overdo it, causing the horse to turn in.) The whip may be used to touch but never hit the horse. Never put your whip down: bending down to pick it up could be risky from the point of view of control as well as your own safety. If the horse is fresh, you can hold the lash and keep the whip very quiet and low.

It is important that the lunge rein is looped safely and not twisted. Practise coiling it so that it won't tighten around your hand or allow you to put a foot through it. The rein should come out of the top of your hand towards the horse. Handling the rein and whip are best practised well away from the horse. Try aiming the lash at a fence post until you have perfected the necessary 'flick of the wrist'.

Start by allowing the horse to loosen up in walk and then trot on both reins. Do not fit the side reins straightaway, unless essential for control and safety.

The bulk of the work will be in trot, with short spells of relaxation in walk and changes of rein about every five minutes. Transitions will help develop suppleness and agility. Some work in canter can be beneficial, but only if the horse remains calm and should not be attempted by an inexperienced handler or before the horse shows good balance in trot.

Conclude the work with a few minutes' walk without side reins, encouraging the horse to stretch down and relax.

Lungeing the Rider The basis of effective riding is an independent seat which means that you can

Top
Relaxing forward into a light contact with side reins, which are attached to the girth straps. The next stage will be to ask for rather more activity.

Top right
Make sure that the stirrup irons are secured before asking the horse to work.

Above
This horse is being lunged in a roller as an alternative to a saddle. The cavesson is a little too large and would be more comfortable if it fitted under the cheekpieces. The horse is 'falling in' on the circle, causing the lunge rein to slacken.

Overleaf
Ridden lessons on the lunge are particularly useful for riders wishing to improve their position and seat.

remain in balance in all three paces without relying on the reins for support or gripping with the legs.

Lungeing allows riders to concentrate on developing their own balance, suppleness and security while someone else controls the horse. It is valuable at all levels and an ideal way of improving the rider's position and helping them develop 'feel' for the horse's movement. Lungeing can help inexperienced riders gain confidence and is suitable for all other than small children who usually prefer close contact with the teacher and the extra security that a lesson on the leading rein affords. The right sort of horse is important – steady and comfortable for the novice, more active and powerful for the experienced.

Usually the horse is lunged in walk and trot, although canter may be used with experienced riders. Being lunged is tiring for both horse and rider, so lessons should not be longer than half-an-hour. Lungeing is a good opportunity to work without stirrups to deepen and strengthen the seat. It is important that your instructor has a good eye and can see past the symptoms to the root cause of any fault. There are all sorts of bending, stretching and loosening exercises that will help, but you need to choose the right ones for you.

Lungeing equipment Only lunge in a mild, comfortably fitting snaffle bit. Remove bridle noseband, secure or remove reins.

You will require a lungeing cavesson, fitted snugly either just above, or with certain cavessons, below the bit. Your saddle should have its stirrups secured or removed. If removed, use a surcingle to secure the saddle flaps. A lungeing roller with D rings set at several levels can also be used. You will also require side reins.

The lunge rein is usually made from webbing, with swivel attachment and strong clip. Nylon webbing is more difficult to handle. The lunge whip should be as long as possible while remaining light and well balanced.

Never lunge a horse without putting brushing-boots on all four legs. It is a good idea to use over-reach boots as well.

The lungeing cavesson There are various types of cavesson available; most fit above the bit, inside the cheekpieces; the noseband should fit firmly and without pinching. Make sure that it doesn't rub the cheek-bones or pinch the lips between the noseband and bit.

The jowl strap should fit firmly around the bottom of the cheek-bone to prevent the cheekpieces slipping towards the horse's eyes. If too near the throat the effect is lost and discomfort is caused, interfering with the horse's ability to flex.

Some cavessons fit as a 'drop' noseband, the lower strap fastening under the bit. Care must be taken to ensure the nosepiece does not interfere with the breathing and that the lower strap fits snugly without pinching.

Side reins There are various types made from nylon or leather, with or without rubber rings or elastic inserts to allow some 'give' if the horse is startled or upset. Elastic that stretches too easily encourages the horse to lean on the reins.

To check that the reins are of a suitable length, position the horse's head and neck in a rounded 'novice' outline. The side reins should reach in this position and have room for adjustment both ways.

If the horse is accustomed to being lunged, measure and adjust 2.5 cm (1 inch) longer. If not, adjust very loosely. Attach to the girth straps under both and then back under the first to avoid them slipping down, or to the rings on the lungeing roller.

Never attach side reins to saddle and bit or cavesson when the horse is stabled or tied. When adjusted, clip them to the D rings on the front of the saddle.

When lungeing, the handler on the ground should wear a well-secured hard hat, gloves and sensible footwear.

Lungeing should ideally take place in a confined space such as a fenced arena or indoor school. The corner of a field, if safely fenced, can be adapted, preferably with the open sides contained by a safe temporary barrier, such as poles on large oil drums.

The surface should be level, even, non-slip, neither hard- nor deep-going. In bad weather, a straw or wood-chip ring may provide a temporary solution.

Lungeing technique You should lunge in a circle of approximately 15 m (50 ft) in diameter, but for a young or unbalanced horse, start with a larger

one of up to 20 m (65 ft). For more experienced and supple horses the circle can for short spells be made smaller.

Lungeing times vary according to the horse's ability, ranging from 5–10 minutes of mostly walking with a young or unfit horse, to up to 40 minutes when exercising or working a very fit one. The average time in most situations will be 20 minutes of actual work. Remember, lungeing is a very strenuous exercise, so take care that your horse isn't being over-stretched.

Once the horse understands and accepts the basic idea of walking and trotting actively on the circle you can introduce the side reins. These help maintain control and attention, especially in the case of an exuberant animal. They also help develop straightness and balance, discouraging the horse from falling in or out with the shoulders or turning his head away from the line of the circle. They encourage the horse to accept a light contact with the bit, stretching his top line and carrying himself in a rounded, balanced outline. As a result, he will start to develop the correct muscles and a supple swinging back and gradually learn to work actively forward onto the bit.

Side reins should be attached no lower than the horizontal when the horse's head is in the required position. They should not be allowed

to slip down as they could bear down on the bars of the mouth and possibly cause a sensitive horse to panic.

Never lead a horse to and from the stable with side reins attached. Check that they are both the same length and do not leave a horse standing with only one attached; unclip both before adjusting the length. Fasten side reins onto the bit rings below the bridle reins.

The side reins should initially be long, exerting only a slight influence on the horse's outline. As the horse becomes accustomed to them they can be shortened gradually until they are of such a length that the horse, working actively forward, is encouraged to stretch his neck forward and seek a contact with the bit, relaxing at the jaw and poll and gradually carrying his head nearer to, but always slightly in front of the vertical when trotting. Because side reins are fixed, few horses will pull against them, learning instead to take up a light contact with the bit. They must never be shortened to such a degree that the head and neck are forced into a position when there will be discomfort, stiffening of the back, and restriction of the shoulders and stride. Do not walk the horse for prolonged periods with side reins attached as, unless they are very long, they will restrict freedom of movement.

Chapter Twelve
JUMPING

Jumping should be fun for both horse and rider and its enjoyment is all to do with confidence in yourself and one another.

The rider's position and suppleness are of utmost importance. A balanced position will not only help you to feel safe but enable you to influence the horse effectively.

The key factors are a strong, secure lower leg position and the ability to 'fold' with the horse over the fence. Shortening the stirrup leathers (generally by at least two holes, often more) makes this mechanically easier. The exact length depends on your body proportions, your leg shape and to some extent the saddle you are using. If the stirrups are too short you may be top heavy, unbalanced and unable to use your legs effectively. If they are too long your seat will become weak and insecure.

Between fences, the upper body should be inclined slightly forward (shoulders approximately over knees), the hips moving slightly back and the weight down into the legs, the thighs and seat resting lightly on the saddle. From this position you can sit in and ride firmly if you need to but still go with the horse when he takes off. Some people prefer a more upright position. This can work for an experienced rider but a novice will find it hard to react quickly and smoothly enough to go with the horse over the fence.

The hips, knees and ankles act as shock absorbers, the angles made by the joints closing to absorb the movement. All three need to work together. The heels should be pressed well down, a little more weight down the inside of the leg into the foot, helping to keep the whole leg close to the horse's side.

Try not to grip or press the knee too tight to the saddle, creating a pivot point which causes your lower leg to fly backwards as you jump.

To go with the movement over the fence the upper body must 'fold' forward at the hip (rather than bending at the waist), closing the angle between body and thigh. A straight but relaxed back makes this easier. A rounded back and hips makes it hard to fold and go with the horse. Tensing and hollowing can put the rider too far forward with the hands drawing back, but may equally cause them to get left behind.

As the shoulders move forward the hips need to slide back enough to keep the rider in balance

Practise jumps in the school at home. Try to include fillers of different colours to accustom your horse to brightly-coloured jumps.

Top
The horse has met the poles correctly and is well-balanced and active. The rider is maintaining a sympathetic contact but is a fraction behind the movement.

Above
In the correct jumping position you should find a stirrup length which is short enough for you to fold forward in comfortable balance, but long enough for you to be able to use your legs effectively. Your ankles, knees and hips must remain flexible to act as shock-absorbers. Practise folding your upper body forward in halt. Your hands will be further forward than when riding on the flat, with correspondingly shorter reins.

Opposite
Ouch! The rider has launched himself up and forward and is trying to 'lift' the horse over the fence with unfortunate consequences for his poor mount.

over the leg. The lower leg must stay in place, not swing back or brace forward as the rider moves his body.

As the horse takes off, the thrust of the jump will fold you automatically if you are sitting correctly and are relaxed. The bigger and more powerful the jump, the more obvious this will be.

A well-balanced saddle, of sufficient forward cut and not too high in the cantle, makes all this much easier.

The hand should follow a straight line down to the bit allowing the horse maximum freedom without losing the contact. This can be tricky, especially for a novice rider. The 'crest release', where the hands follow the stretch of the crest is an effective option.

Tension in the shoulders and arms will affect the rider's ability to allow with his hands, even if his position appears balanced. On the other hand, a firm or even strong contact need not stop you from going with the movement. Try to avoid drawing back or suddenly allowing just before the fence. Keeping your hands low (but not fixed down) with a bend in your elbows helps them to follow naturally as the horse stretches his head and neck over the fence. Your hands will be further forward than when riding on the flat, with correspondingly shorter reins. Too-long a rein encourages the hands to draw back, too-short makes it hard to allow sufficiently.

Despite our best endeavours everyone gets 'left behind' occasionally. If in doubt, hang onto the mane or neck strap. It is also a good idea to

practise opening your fingers and slipping the reins to avoid catching the horse in the mouth. The horse's jumping style is also important.

A horse judges the take-off point in front of a jump by looking down at the base-line. He won't be able to do this if his head is too high or the rein aid too strong. A well-filled fence with a solid ground-line under or just in front will always be easier to jump than a solitary pole. A 'false' ground-line behind rather than under the front poles can cause a horse to misjudge and hit the fence.

Over the fence, the horse needs to be free to stretch his head and neck, lift his shoulders and use his back muscles to produce the rounded shape or 'bascule' which is the hallmark of a good jumper. In this shape he can fold his legs well beneath him, clearing the fences more easily. A horse that jumps in a hollow shape with his head up will usually dangle his legs and either hit the fence or have to jump exaggeratedly high to clear it. It is most uncomfortable for the horse and the rider.

It is easy to forget the importance of the horse and rider's balance after the fence. On landing, the rider's legs absorb the movement and the body straightens up. The legs stay close to the horse, ready to send him forward into the hands which keep or regain a quiet contact with no snatches or jerks. It is important not to sit back too soon, causing the horse to hollow and drop his hind-legs onto the fence. Getting in front of the movement will mean lack of security and control, and the rider will probably end up leaning on their hands in order to keep their balance.

Where the rider looks is even more crucial when jumping than on the flat. 'You end up where you look' is a well-proven maxim. Look up and ahead, at the top rail or over the fence you are approaching. While still in mid-air, start looking towards the next fence or turn. Never look into the bottom of the jump or behind you to see if you have knocked down a pole.

It may seen obvious that you should focus on what is ahead of you but it is easy to momentarily lose concentration after a particularly good or bad jump.

The Approach Meet the centre of the jump square on, the horse's body, shoulders and neck straight. Maintain an even elastic contact and steady speed. Maintain the rhythm, especially if adjusting the stride length. Look ahead at the top of the fence or over to the next jump. Sit quietly, your legs close to the horse's side, clearly, however gently, saying 'go forward'.

Avoid interfering at the last minute, particularly by using the whip: unless your timing is exact you will simply distract the horse. Try not to tip your upper body forward or give your hands suddenly in front of the fence. Avoid drawing your hands back and up on take-off, trying to 'lift' the horse over the fence, as this hollows and restricts him. Don't kick: this wastes energy and the horse may duck sideways or stop while your legs are off

his sides in between kicks. Don't shove with your seat: this will hollow the horse's back.

Horses need to know where they are with you. Be as consistent as possible in the way you ride. A typical example is the rider who 'hooks back' and puts the horse in close to the fence all the time and then suddenly sees a long stride and asks the horse to stand off the fence without warning. This is asking for a stop or a demolition job. You may have wondered how a clumsy rider can still manage to regularly jump a clear round. This is because a generous horse has become accustomed to his rider's mistakes and learned to take care of himself. In this case, being consistently bad is better than being inconsistent. This isn't to suggest that bad riding is a recipe for success!

Everyone can improve their technique and ability: you may only need a few minor adjustments but if you are plainly unhappy with your jumping it is worth going back to stage one and starting again from scratch.

On the other hand, if you have been jumping for some time and are getting results and enjoying yourself, be wary of making sudden changes. It takes time to adjust mentally and physically to a different way of doing things and trying to change overnight could easily destroy your confidence. The same applies to the horse who will have become used to you. It helps to have a trainer whom you trust to give you confidence when you are learning new things. It is easy to lose your

'feel' when you are thinking hard about what you are doing, so be kind to yourself and take your time. Make changes gradually and don't make great demands on the horse until you are both happily in harmony and riding instinctively again.

Practice is important, both to build up your strength and develop suppleness. The same applies to developing an 'eye for a stride'. Some people have a natural instinct for this but the rest of us need to work at it. Be fair to yourself. If you rarely jump you are bound to be a bit stiff and creaky and slow to react. A couple of jumping sessions a week is reasonable while you and your horse are learning. You may find it better to jump a few fences most days, or to occasionally school over fences for three to four days in a row before having a break. Be aware that from the horse's point of view, being over-jumped is worse than doing too little and can lead to a jaded unenthusiastic animal, physically and mentally over-stressed. If you are competing regularly you may not need to practise at all unless you come across a problem that needs working on.

Hard, uneven ground and heavy going will cause jarring or strains, so try to keep jumping to a minimum. However, it is unwise to only ever practise jumping in a surfaced arena before going out to compete on grass. You and the horse need some practice to get used to both the different surface and the wider open spaces. You could find that your horse dislikes a firmer surface or finds the extra space so exciting that he nearly pulls your arms out. On the other hand, he may come to life with just that perfect extra sparkle.

Be careful not to do too much in one session (better to stop while you both feel you'd like to jump a few more fences) and take care to build up the sessions progressively (imagine how you'd feel after an over-enthusiastic keep-fit session!).

You can learn a lot without actually leaving the ground. Pole-work will enliven flat-work sessions and you can work on your jumping position when schooling and while hacking. This is especially important for riding cross-country: try gradually increasing the length of time you stay off the horse's back in forward position while you trot or canter.

Jumping needs a basis of good flat work. The difficult part is getting to the fence in balance at the right speed and with enough energy. If you can do that, the jump itself becomes relatively easy. To jump well, the horse needs to have a particularly well-balanced canter, rounded and to the bit, light in the forehand, the hind-legs carrying more of the bodyweight. He should react immediately to your legs both to go forward and turn and be able to ` lengthen and shorten his stride with ease, maintaining the same even rhythm as he does so.

Try to develop an active, medium-length stride with the feeling that the horse is keen to go forward but attentive and prepared to be contained without an argument. This will give you confidence and you will also find it easier to 'see' a stride and ride from fence to fence in a steady rhythm without having to make major adjustments before each jump. Watch the fence coming towards you and if necessary either contain the

Here the rider is in front of the movement which has made her insecure, causing her lower leg to swing back and away from the horse.

Below
This horse is careful with his fore-legs because the cross-pole is higher on the right, causing him to lift his off-fore higher. The rider is standing in the stirrups, rather than folding, but is not interfering with the horse's freedom over the fence.

Opposite
Both horse and rider have completely missed the stride and have taken off much too close. However, they are both making a big effort to retrieve the situation.

canter or allow the horse to open up a little to meet the fence correctly.

In general, it is better, especially with small fences, to ask the horse to go in a little deeper, encouraging a rounder stride and jump rather than getting into the habit of standing the horse off further and further from the fences.

There is nothing worse than a canter which lacks energy or is 'stuck in a groove' on one non-adjustable stride length. The answer is to improve the basic flat work, getting a sharper response to the leg and making the horse more supple with lots of transitions and speed up/slow down within the pace.

The horse may have a naturally slow rhythm. Be careful not to chase it out of balance, confusing impulsion with speed. Concentrate on creating energy and lightening the forehand. As long as they have plenty of impulsion, horses need surprisingly little speed to jump over a high fence. This type of horse can make up for its lack of speed by learning to turn well.

An excitable horse will need calm, quiet riding with an emphasis on rhythm. Meeting the horse half-way is often the key. Better to be slightly quick but in harmony than fighting all the way.

A very short canter stride is fine for accurately jumping uprights, but you need a good eye and a responsive horse to be able to open up the stride to give enough scope to clear a large parallel. The rider needs tact and experience as the horse will be relying very much on their judgement. One common fault is to 'hook back' until you see a stride and then frantically kick for the fence. This very quickly teaches a keen horse to fight and anticipate and charge at the fence on his forehand.

Riding on too-long and 'downhill' a stride, with the horse all strung out, makes it hard to balance through the turns or to meet the fence at the right take-off point. If you are also travelling too fast, then life becomes even more difficult and possibly downright dangerous. A clever horse will respond by putting in a short stride in front of the fence, adjusting its balance enough to allow it to clear the fence. A less confident animal, realizing at the last moment that its weight is too far forward, will stop or duck out. A horse with power and scope may well take off further and further away until eventually it hits the fence with possible disastrous consequences.

If you feel uncomfortable when jumping, try this checklist: Do you tense or hold your breath? Try counting or singing out loud on the approach. Do you get left behind the movement on the take-off?; this will result in your being catapulted up the horse's neck on landing. If you are in front of the movement on the approach and take-off, you won't catch the horse in the mouth but you will be unable to prevent a last-minute hesitation and may well go straight over his head if he stops. This often goes with the lower leg swinging too far back. Having the lower leg rather far forward can be a secure 'safety first' position but, if it goes with stiff hips and legs and a round back, the rider will tend to get 'left behind' and be unable to use their legs effectively.

Getting results Your attitude is crucial: your enthusiasm and commitment can transform a hesitant or disinterested horse. Equally, if you are nervous yourself, it transmits itself instantly to the horse and it is not uncommon to see a horse make a refusal when it was pretty obvious that the rider had stopped several strides before.

Horses which lack confidence will benefit from jumping the same fences several times and you should be particularly careful to increase the height gradually. If you change the appearance of a fence, make it lower until the horse is used to it. With this type of horse, always start several stages back from where you finished last time.

With a lively horse, don't repeat the same exercise too often as it will wind him up. Vary the track and change the type of fence or filler to make him think. Place poles on the ground between the elements of combinations to help with the horse's stride. Intersperse flat work with the occasional jump, working in and out of the jumps so that he learns to settle and not anticipate. (This works well in reverse to brighten up a horse which is becoming bored with flat work.)

A bold horse will get careless if the fences are too low. Warming up gradually is still important but, after trotting and cantering a low practice jump a few times, it will be better to jump more challenging fences. This type of horse can become over-excited jumping lines of fences with related distances and will settle better if the work involves many changes of direction (not tight turns). Concentrate on maintaining the rhythm of the pace and riding a really good track and you will find the jumps take care of themselves.

One of the most important moments with any type of horse is landing and riding away from the fence. The rider needs to be supple and balanced enough to organize the horse's balance and rhythm from the first stride after landing. This takes practice – count how many strides it takes you to be actually riding again – probably two or three. A strong horse will get progressively more onward-bound after each fence and a lazy one will almost grind to a halt if you are not ready and waiting to react.

Control is essential when jumping: better to circle away in plenty of time than have an accident, but avoid pulling the horse out at the last minute as he may lose balance, certainly lose confidence in you, and learn how to 'duck out' at a fence.

If you are committed to the fence, keep your leg round the horse, asking him to keep his hocks under him and keeping your rein contact. Keep your body in place and your hands down; try not to be pulled forward. Leaning back with your

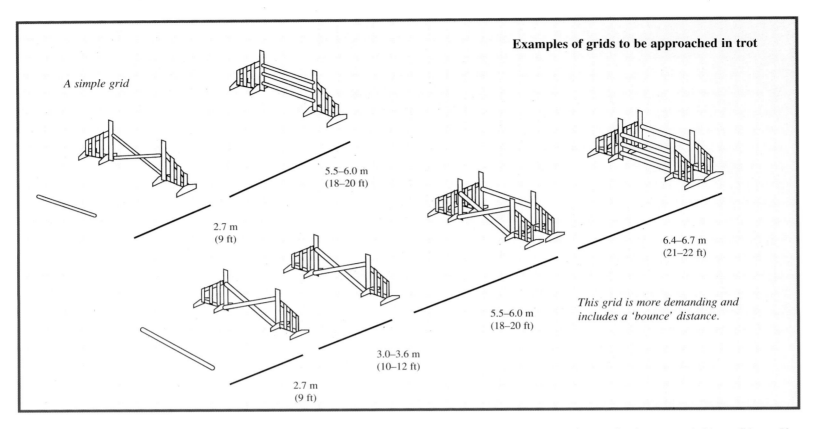

Examples of grids to be approached in trot

A simple grid

5.5–6.0 m (18–20 ft)

2.7 m (9 ft)

6.4–6.7 m (21–22 ft)

This grid is more demanding and includes a 'bounce' distance.

5.5–6.0 m (18–20 ft)

3.0–3.6 m (10–12 ft)

2.7 m (9 ft)

hands up will hollow the horse's back, make him resist more, and it is more likely that he will hit the fence. The higher his head, the harder it is for him to see the fence, round his back and fold his legs sufficiently to clear it. Try not to 'drop' the contact, suddenly 'giving' with the hands immediately in front of the fence. Even if the horse has no intention of stopping it will disrupt his balance at just the wrong moment. A horse that lacks confidence and is rushing from fear may very well stop dead if he suddenly loses you. If the horse is backing off an intimidating fence you will need a firm seat, quiet, steady hands, and strong, quiet leg aids. Kicking doesn't work – the leg is off the horse's side more than on it and usually at just the moment he decides to duck out.

Riders sometimes get a fixation over a particular fence. Common reactions are to be too careful, adjusting and interfering too much, to dramatically over-ride or to sit there and freeze. Initially, practise over small versions with the help of a good instructor. Visualization can help: if your horse always hits gates but clears parallels easily, put on an imaginary back pole behind the gate and ride a parallel. If you know you have a tendency to freeze, riding a little stronger than usual and really looking up and ahead will help; but don't start kicking and flapping. As with everything to do with jumping, improve your flat work. The more balanced and adjustable the canter, the easier everything will seem.

At shows If you are nervous, and it is not just competition butterflies, opt for an easier class (even if others try to persuade you otherwise). There is no point risking your confidence and possibly causing your horse to lose his. Build up

gradually until the smaller fences become boring, then move up a grade. Jumping in two classes means that you can try the bigger fences after a practice over smaller ones. Don't be tempted to jump in too many classes though, as your horse will get either more excited and careless or bored and tired and may start to refuse.

Jumping Problems

General checks If your horse fails to jump well at first, check that he is comfortable. Look for badly-fitting tack; a bit that is too severe, sharp teeth, or discomfort (if not obvious lameness) from his feet, legs or back. Does he appear to dislike hard, heavy or slippery going? Make sure you are in balance, effective and fit enough. A more experienced rider may be able to gain the horse's respect and confidence enabling you to carry on the good work.

The horse that rushes He may be keen and enthusiastic but could equally be afraid and attempting to get the dreaded event over as soon as possible. Either way he must be persuaded to make a calmer, more balanced approach. When riding him, don't encourage speed. A horse that rushes can be improved with flat work which will gain you more control. When jumping, don't fix your hands and pull on the approach, try to *half-halt* with the stride. Avoid too strong a check straight after landing, the horse may well run away more in anticipation of a jab in the mouth.

Don't allow yourself to tip forward on the approach or landing but equally avoid leaning back fighting. Try not to over-check: the horse may fight you because he feels you won't give him the freedom to jump. If he is actually afraid, try

jumping smaller fences to gain his confidence. If he is too bold, don't repeat the same fence time after time so that he gets careless and rushes even more. Finally, if he hits a fence and rushes away, pat and reassure him.

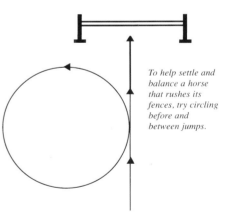

To help settle and balance a horse that rushes its fences, try circling before and between jumps.

Keep the horse bending around the circle until you have established a steady rhythm and he has stopped anticipating the jump. Straighten up quietly, letting the horse know that this time you are going to jump, without making any sudden changes in your position or aids. Try to keep the rhythm and speed constant.

Try these exercises to gain his confidence.
- Work over and round scattered single poles.
- Jump one or two fences interspersed with flat-work schooling.
- Circle between or before fences.

fence. Low, gently-sloping cross-poles guide a novice horse or rider to the centre of the fence, but if the horse veers to the side he is forced to jump a higher part of it. A steep-sided cross-pole encourages the horse to use his shoulders and lift and fold his fore-legs. Ascending spread fences will help the horse to open up and stretch over the fence while a true parallel demands physical effort and athleticism and will encourage the horse to lift his shoulders and use his back muscles to produce a rounded shape (bascule) over the fence.

After a spread fence the horse will tend to go on the forehand. Practise riding spread to upright or upright to spread on a related distance (containing the energy or moving the horse on a little). Try different types of fence after a turn. Practise a narrow fence three or four strides after a normal one (concentrating on rhythm and straightness). To encourage the horse to land on the correct leg and be ready for a tight turn after the fence, turn your upper body in mid-air and look in the direction you wish to go. Open the inner rein a little, taking care not to pull back and keep the outer rein to the neck.

As you gain experience you can practise jumping upright fences at an angle to save time in a jump-off. *(This is discussed in the next chapter.)* Jumping a spread at an angle increases the width and should generally be avoided. Gates and planks will tip and fall more easily if the horse touches them with a hoof.

The lazy horse Try a canter rather than a trot approach when jumping grids, but take care that the distances are suitable. Practise improving the response to the leg aids, using a stick if necessary. Improve the horse's suppleness and do spells of strong canter on the flat. Ride for activity rather than speed and try to motivate him: you could try sponsored rides or cross-country with another horse. Constantly repeating the same jump causes boredom and carelessness.

Refusals If the horse hesitates, keep riding firmly up to a contact. Don't look for a stride – keep pressing forward as though you mean to canter straight through the fence.

After a refusal, and if you are sure it was mere naughtiness, use your stick behind your leg immediately. There is no point turning the horse away from the fence and then scolding it.

Give yourself room to get the horse going forward again and make sure of a straight approach. Charging at the fence rarely works: it is better to keep the horse fairly steady, riding positively forward into a contact and ready to give stronger aids if required.

Run-outs Check that the horse is in balance, not on the forehand or travelling too fast. Ride forward positively but steadily, keeping the horse straight, and check that your line is correct. Carry your whip the side the horse wants to run out (give him a light tap behind the leg or on the shoulder to remind him). Think of your reins as a tunnel and push the horse between them. If the horse tries to run left, keep your left hand near the neck; open your right hand away from the neck. (Don't bend the horse's neck to the right, making it easier for him to duck out onto the left shoulder.) Sit up a

little more than usual.

Occasionally you may be more successful if you trot the fence, especially if the horse was scared by it, but you must be thinking forward all the time. Try to turn the horse the opposite way from the way it wants to go. (If it ran out left, turn it around to the right before retracing your steps rather than continuing to circle left.)

Jumping courses To ride a course well you need a feel for the right rhythm and speed, the ability to ride a good track, and an eye for a stride. Be in control but in partnership; if you are over-dominant the horse will be unable to help you should you make a mistake.

Although jumping single fences and grids is important in training, practising courses is also necessary. It is one thing to jump one or two fences in perfect style, quite another to put ten together without an error.

To find the correct 'line' to the fence, look ahead from mid-air over the previous jump. Keep looking towards it from well before you start to turn. Aim to be square onto the centre. Place the horse's shoulders in line, using both reins and legs. On turns it is better to have a slightly incorrect bend than the horse falling through the outside shoulder with too much bend.

Try practising with a course marked out with cones or wings: ride through the gaps in trot and then canter. Try trotting over a course made up of single poles on the ground.

If you only have a small number of jumps, you can still practise the situations you are likely to meet in competition. A 'tunnel' of poles and markers will help your steering.

Remember to practise different types of

Distances

In show-jumping these are based on a stride of 3.6 m (12 ft). Your horse may have a stride that is naturally shorter or longer than this. When schooling you may initially have to adjust the distances to keep his confidence, but you should work to encourage him to take a standard length stride. 1.8 m (6ft) is allowed for take-off and for landing. The elements of a double or treble will be approximately 7.3 m (24 ft) apart for one stride and 10.4–11 m (34–36 ft) for two. Distances will be shorter if the fences are small (down to 6.3–6.6 m (21–22 ft) for a one-stride double. Distances will also vary a little according to the type of fence. For example, because a horse lands further out over a triple bar the comfortable distance to an upright fence following it will be longer than average. Indoors and uphill distances will be shorter, downhill a little longer. 'Related distances' refer to fences spaced from 3–8 strides apart. For novice horses only 'true' distances should be used.

Exercises to try

Poles can be used in all sorts of ways to help horse and rider, both on the flat and when jumping. You can ride over poles with either flat-work or jumping-length stirrups. Be careful not to ride too long or your joints won't be able to absorb the extra spring the poles generate in the horse's stride.

Poles help the rider by improving balance, suppleness and strength, focusing the attention on controlling straightness, rhythm, and accuracy. In other words, you can't get away with allowing the horse to drift slightly off-line or alter his rhythm or stride length and still negotiate the poles successfully. They help the horse by improving his awareness of where he is putting his feet, as well as his agility, suppleness and rhythm.

As he goes over the poles he will need to lift his feet higher, flexing his joints more in the process. He should be encouraged to stretch over his back and top line, rounding his frame and looking forward and down at the poles.

Most horses enjoy pole work. Some find it exciting, others worrying to start with, but it should calm the horse's approach to jumping long-term and is excellent as a first introduction to jumping. It also teaches the horse and rider to make small adjustments to the length of stride in order to meet the poles at the correct point and in rhythm.

For safety's sake, take progressive steps. Start with one pole and build up gradually as the horse gains confidence. Never start again with pole work or a grid of fences where you left off last session.

Always go back to the beginning when you may find that you are able to progress more quickly this time. The poles should be heavy to minimize rolling and regularly checked to see that they have not been kicked out of position.

It is very important to place the poles at the right distances for both the horse and the pace you are in. Be observant: if the horse can't find a rhythm, do you need to adjust his stride length, activity or rhythm, or are the poles wrongly spaced?

The aim to start with is to cross the poles in the centre at 90°. Start with one pole, first walking over it, then do it in trot. When the horse is calm, try single poles scattered around the arena and gradually cross them at various angles.

Once the horse is happily negotiating single poles in trot, you can build up a line of poles. Start either with 3 poles spaced 1.35–1.55 m (4½–5 ft) apart or two or three 2.7–3 m (9–10 ft) apart. Two poles at the narrower distance might encourage the horse to jump over them. Make sure you stay with the movement and allow with your hands without losing the contact. Should the horse rush or try to canter, circle away and establish a calmer rhythm before trying again. You can try a walk approach, trotting calmly just before or over the first poles. Don't walk over trot poles – the spacing will be wrong.

Try trotting a line of poles spaced 2.7–3 m (9–10 ft) apart. Once the horse is happy with this exercise, try varying the spacing to make it slightly shorter or longer and practise adjusting the horse's stride to match.

Gymnastic Jumping

The place pole This is to guide the horse to the correct take-off point and can be very helpful. Several trotting poles in front of a fence can help promote rhythm, suppleness and concentration. Allow 2.7 m (9 ft) between the nearest pole and the fence.

If ridden positively, poles placed in front of the fence can help improve both the hesitant horse and one that rushes. But they can also be too much to think about for a novice horse or rider. Cantering over trotting poles is dangerous: circle away and re-establish a calm trot before trying again. If the horse canters just in front of a single place pole set for trot, do not pull back or suddenly wrench him away from the jump. Contain the canter as best you can while still quietly riding forward.

A tunnel of poles can be used to keep the horse straight on the approach and landing. The 'v' of the poles will help correct a horse that jumps to one side of the fence.

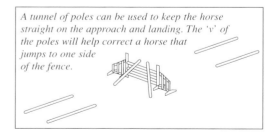

Grids and combinations These develop both horse and rider's athleticism. Build up gradually, initially keeping the fences small. When you add a fence behind an existing one the horse may hesitate, so be ready to ride more positively from the start.

For safety's sake, check your distances: use a tape measure until you are sure 'your' strides are accurate. Only use heavy poles for ground work, (they should not roll) and paint them a bright colour so that the horse can see them easily.

Remove from the wings any jump cups which are not in use. Don't stand near jumps when a horse is jumping and take care with the siting of fences; remember the horse may think that the fence of the arena is part of the course. If you use cavaletti, never pile them up and remember that even single ones could cause a horse to trip.

Learning to 'see' a stride Some people are fortunate in having a natural instinct for this, but for the majority, plenty of practice is required.

Try to let the fence come towards you. Some count and picture the horse's stride covering the ground in front of them. Others find that developing a subconscious *feel* works better.

Here are some exercises you can try. Put two fences two or three strides apart (later up to six). The first fence should be very small with a place pole in front. Approach in trot so that you don't

have to worry about finding a stride to the first fence. Ride even-length canter strides to the second fence.

Because of the trot approach, the distances will be shorter than standard. In general 9 m (30 ft) for two strides works well, encouraging the horse to use himself and not race on between fences. For each extra stride between fences add another 3.6 m (12 ft). If the second fence is very low, or your horse hesitant or short-striding, you may need to shorten the distances by up to 0.45 m (1ft 6 inches) per stride to start with.

Once you are confident, try cantering two fences which are the standard distance apart. If you start with the first fence very low you may need to shorten the total distance by 0.6–1 m 2–3 ft. Aim for even strides but be ready to steady or push on if necessary. React quickly so that you can adjust all the strides a little rather than taking, say, three long ones, followed by a frantic check. You can also jump fences after turns or half-circles until you can picture how many strides will bring you to the take-off point.

Chapter Thirteen
CROSS-COUNTRY

This should be fun. Make sure you do your groundwork properly and work on your flat work and gymnastic jumping before you start serious schooling. It is worth the wait because a responsive, balanced, horse is a joy to ride cross-country and is more likely to stay happy and sound. There is a great deal of pleasure to be had from playing with a young horse over a variety of tiny fences and a good introduction would be any small logs you come across when hacking out. It is important to avoid getting the horse over-excited and deciding that all fences should be jumped from a gallop! Jumping fixed fences at speed on a horse which jumps flat and hasn't reached the required level of agility and learned to lift his undercarriage is neither safe nor enjoyable.

Riding cross-country should be a partnership. Nurture the horse's ability to think for himself, when needed. When schooling, jump steadily until you both feel confident; but remember that you both need to learn to jump at speed before you compete. As with show-jumping, maintaining the right rhythm and speed with the horse in balance is your main aim. The horse can then get on with jumping the fences.

It is neither kind nor safe to ride cross-country in a half-hearted manner. You must be determined and in an absolutely positive frame of mind. If a fence worries you, ride it with extra determination. If you hesitate the horse will feel it – try visualizing the two of you sailing over in perfect style. Remember, be vocal in your encouragement and praise and give a pat on the neck after a special effort.

Unless your horse is actually afraid of the whip, you should always carry one. There is no need to be over-aggressive. Even with a bold horse, an occasional reminder may be necessary and is much safer and kinder to the horse than letting him hesitate and maybe even fall. You may need to recapture the horse's attention after a bad jump to help you organize him before the next fence. When approaching a fence or on take-off, a smack with the stick can encourage a bigger effort or sharper response to your leg aids. The timing is, however, all-important, as using the stick a few strides out can disturb the horse's concentration and make matters worse. It all comes down to experience and feel. Use the whip behind your leg to say 'go forward', and listen. A slap on the shoulder could make the horse veer to the side.

For safety's sake, never jump when you are alone and always check the fences first.

It is important to think of the course as a whole rather than one jump at a time. When you are schooling it helps to put together a group of fences into a mini-course as it is much more encouraging to feel you are going somewhere. Try

not to unnerve the horse by jumping too many difficult fences one after the other and don't be tempted to try that extra big one 'just to see if he can do it'. Your whole aim is to develop the horse's confidence. Decide *never* to have a refusal. To this end you must ride firmly but intelligently and build up the questions you ask in a sensible manner. Start with fences small enough to step over from a standstill. The horse must learn that, whatever happens, he will not be allowed to turn away from a jump.

There will be times when the horse makes an awkward jump. Sometimes it is worth going back to try the fence again but there is a chance that the horse will decide not to risk another unpleasant experience and he will refuse. Often it is better to carry on; get the horse going well over some easier fences and try the difficult one later or leave it to

Opposite
Jumps over water require excellent balance and total commitment is essential.

Above
The rider has been left behind, ballooning out of the saddle, but is making a valiant attempt to allow with the hands.

Right
The author and Alfie riding a trakener fence, wearing brushing- and over-reach boots. A hunting breast plate is used to stop the saddle from slipping back, and an over-girth is fitted over the saddle lying over the girth. It is buckled under the belly where it will not interfere with the horse's elbow or the rider's leg. The reins are knotted together, then buckled, and the bridle headpiece is tied to a plait at the top of the mane. Plaiting up the tail prevents it getting thick and heavy with mud. All these precautions worked when horse and rider had a fall at the previous fence!
(Picture: Martha Shaw)

another occasion.

Getting a lead from another horse can be helpful on occasions but often your horse will not be looking where he is going. Generally speaking, it is better to go back to working over small fences and build up the horse's trust in you.

A strong trot can be the best pace for introducing unusual fences. Practise the transition from gallop to trot, thinking forward and striving to maintain the horse's concentration (he mustn't think he's going to have a little break!).

Keeping your horse on the line you have chosen is not easy but is essential. This is especially important when jumping angled fences, corners and arrowheads. The horse must stay absolutely straight, both on the line and through his whole body into your hands. It can be tempting to let him move a little to the left or right to improve the stride – this can easily end up as a habit and lead to run-outs: practise adjusting the horse's stride instead.

Practise riding away from each fence quickly and smoothly, looking ahead and picking up the line you need to the next jump as soon as possible.

It is useful to practise jumping fences at an angle (slight to start with). In competition it will help you chose the best going or an easier distance through a combination.

When learning to jump these kinds of fences it will help to start with tiny versions on drums or blocks. Bear in mind that if you hit a fence when jumping at an angle you are more likely to fall. Always ride straight if the going is deep or the horse tired.

You can learn a lot from riding at cross-country speed over undulating terrain. Practise keeping your balance going up and down hill and pretend you are approaching imaginary fences. Get a feel of how long it takes you to speed up/slow down and turn. The more even the rhythm, the less it tires the horse. This is also a good time to practise your gallop position. You need to conserve as much of the horse's (and your own) energy as possible in between fences and bumping on the poor animal's back is not the way to achieve this. Your stirrups will probably need to be a little shorter than for show-jumping. Keep the lower leg to the girth, your heels down. There should be a straight line from your elbow to the bit, as always. Think of the contact like playing a fish – neither too strong nor too light. Your seat should be out of the saddle (your conformation

will dictate how much). Try to keep your knees relaxed. Fixed knees create a pivot-point, tipping the lower leg back and the upper body forward.

If you get all this right you will be able to absorb the movement without your shoulders rocking to and fro. You should look and feel still but not stiff.

Riding the fences Your aim is to ride the course as a flowing, rhythmic whole; but you will obviously not be able to jump every fence out of a gallop stride. In between fences, stay off the horse's back in gallop position, allowing him to move freely under you. About six to eight strides

away from the fence (or further back if you need to), sit up and into the saddle, balancing the horse and preparing him for the fence. In general, be careful you don't sit too strongly, causing the horse to hollow. If you feel him hesitate and back off the fence, sit 'behind' him and keep pushing him forward into a contact while making sure you give him plenty of freedom over the fence. Give yourself time to get organized so that you can then positively ride forward to every fence. You don't want to be frantically checking, in effect saying 'stop', just before the take-off point. Some fences need a very steady approach. There is a knack to riding slowly towards a fence but very clearly

Opposite
A strong, balanced position. Greasing the fronts of the horse's legs helps them slide free if he hits a fence, reducing the chance of a fall. If too great an area is covered, however, it slows down the cooling process after work.

Below
The rider has presented the horse to the corner at the correct angle. She is a little in front of the movement and in her efforts to hold him to the line is slightly restricting him over the fence.

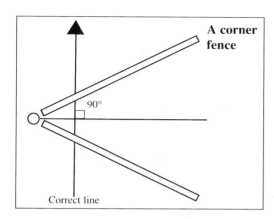

A corner fence

90°

Correct line

saying 'go forward', your legs round the horse sending him into your hands.

When approaching an upright, balance the horse and don't approach it too fast. Spreads can be jumped more out of your natural stride. Precision is needed for very upright parallels and fences, such as hayracks, which give a false ground-line. With combinations, the speed and length of stride will depend on the distances between elements as well as the approach. Keep the horse straight, balanced, and listening to you. Don't approach drop fences fast or flat but with enough momentum for a flowing jump. The horse is less likely to be afraid if he gets a chance to see where he is landing, so avoid asking him to stand off. Landing too fast or steep can both cause loss of balance.

Steps-up require a bouncy canter with plenty of energy and make sure you get your weight sufficiently forward to stay in balance. Steps-down should be approached in an active canter or sometimes a trot. Look up, sit back a little as you go down, lower leg slightly forward, heel deep, close to the horse ready to urge him on should he hesitate. Be ready to slip your reins if necessary.

When riding into or out of woodland, make a steady approach to allow the horse's vision to adjust, and ride him firmly through. Corners and angled fences require absolute control of straightness and a good 'line'. Keep a strong but steady canter and think forward.

To train your horse to jump ditches, start with a dry ditch narrow enough to step over: it should be wide left to right in case the horse tries to swerve out. Progress to larger ditches and then to ones filled with water. When schooling, use a steady trot or canter approach, 'sit behind' any hesitation but get your seat off the saddle to go with him as he takes off. You should aim for a flowing jump. In competition, there are occasions when a strong approach may get you to the other side before the horse has time to realize what he is jumping.

Approach coffins in a steady, very controlled but active canter. At the beginning, gain the horse's confidence by starting with small ditches then adding small movable fences placed at least one stride away, gradually building up to the real thing.

When jumping into water, approach in trot or a bouncy canter and not too fast, as the drag of the water may cause the horse to tip up. Stay in the pace you land in. When negotiating a jump into water, ride strongly but steadily. Sit back on landing, especially if there is a drop, as you may be pitched forward onto the horse's neck. Slip the reins, if necessary, but practise gathering them up again quickly.

When teaching the horse about water, remember that horses are naturally afraid of it if they can't see the bottom. Start with shallow puddles then on to shallow, clear water. The approach should be as wide and as gentle an incline and as firm as possible. Let the horse sniff and investigate; but he must go in. Keep everything as easy as possible. Once they get the idea most horses love paddling but be careful they don't try to roll! Gradually increase the degree of difficulty and start to ride into muddy water, but always with a firm base. If the horse once loses his footing it may take a long time to regain his trust. Little steps in and out look easy but the horse can easily misjudge them coming out, so give a clear aid. Portable jumps are useful for introducing the horse to jumping into, out of, and in the water.

Chapter Fourteen
GOING OUT FOR A RIDE

Riding your horse around the countryside, or along beaches and trails is a wonderful experience. Horses also love to go out for rides and it is a great form of relaxation for them after strenuous schooling and competition. It is also a great way for the rider to get to know his horse and the way it thinks and feels. Hacking is an excellent way to see the countryside and your higher vantage point can afford some unexpected views of landscape and wildlife.

Make sure that you are properly dressed with a hard hat, sensible boots and, if you are inexperienced, a body-protector. Make sure that you can be seen: wear brightly-coloured tops or jackets, or even better, a fluorescent tabard. There is a vast array of fluorescent clothing for both horse and rider on the market such as hat covers, arm-bands and leg wraps, bridle attachments, exercise sheets and boots and you can't use too many for safety's sake.

For most people, hacking will include at least some riding on public roads. Try to minimize the dangers by avoiding the busiest times of day and stick to quiet roads with no blind bends, if possible. Do not hack if visibility is poor due to fog or heavy rain or in strong winds – even the calmest horse may be alarmed by flying debris.

You are generally safer in company. If you have to hack alone, or your horse gets excited in company, then it is all the more important to always let someone know where you are going and when you are likely to return.

Unfortunately today's roads are mostly unsuitable for riding horses despite the fact that most of us do spend a considerable amount of time on them. Even on quiet country lanes you are bound to meet the occasional road-hog travelling far too fast, and an alarming number of motorists appear to have no idea of a horse's reactions to traffic. Despite this, try to be

considerate yourself and thank motorists who slow down or stop for you.

It is usually safer to ride in single file but 'defensively'. That is, a couple of feet out from the curb to make a bigger obstacle. Ride two abreast with young horses, those nervous in traffic, and young or inexperienced riders who need a steady experienced horse between them and the traffic. You will still need to go in single file around tight bends and along narrow winding roads – usually with the less experienced horse behind – but the young horse will also gain considerable confidence from the presence of a friend behind him, especially if he is nervous of traffic coming from behind. It is worth remembering that quite a few horses that will confidently ignore heavy traffic on a wide road will feel trapped in a narrow lane with hedges and try to whip round or climb into the hedge when a large vehicle approaches.

Keep alert and don't let the horse dawdle; ride

actively forward, keeping contact with the horse's mouth. Look and listen for traffic and other hazards coming from the sides of the road such as plastic bags caught in a hedge, dogs which suddenly jump out barking, anything white, anything that flaps, wet logs which look like monsters: the list is endless.

Discuss with your companions in advance where you are going and at what speed; which horses are better in front or behind, both on roads and in the countryside. Is there one that might kick if crowded or that gets unsettled if not allowed to go in front? Ideally, we should all train our horses to go both in front or behind and at exactly the pace we choose. Intelligent forethought will help you to avoid all sorts of problems.

Try to balance the amount of work you do on your hack. At the start, give the horses at least 10 minute's walk to warm up and then alternate spells of all three paces, depending on the terrain and the going. If your horse is especially excitable in company he may be reluctant to slow up, even when he is tired: it is therefore important that you take note of how much he is 'blowing' and insist that he rests before he overstresses himself. Keep a careful eye on the going: heavy going is always

tiring and cantering suddenly into a patch of it could well result in a lost shoe or a sprain or overreach, or even cause the horse to come down. Hard rutted ground throws strain onto the horse's joints and, along with hard stony gravel, leads to bruised feet. Tractor ruts can be a problem as the horse could injure his back if a hind-leg jolts down into one. Although it is wise not to overdo fast work when the ground is hard, a smooth surface and gentle uphill incline will do the least damage. Wet weather means that the going gets slippery. This is particularly pronounced when rain falls on short grass and hard ground, so avoid turning sharply.

It is important not to always use the same spot for cantering, though this is tempting if there are few other suitable places. Horses unfortunately learn all too quickly and will begin to charge off whether you want them to or not. Try to come back to trot or walk well before the end of the stretch. In any case, never canter or gallop directly towards the approach to a main road. Make sure you are walking in good time before any gate or narrow opening and, if your horse is strong or excitable, only canter where you know you have room for manoeuvre and plenty of time to pull up.

The Nervous Horse

It is perfectly natural for horses to shy. In the wild it is their defence mechanism against predators and sudden dangers. A sharp reaction could be the difference between life and death. These reactions are instinctive: as far as the horse is concerned a rustle in the hedge or a dark shadow could be a tiger about to pounce. When the horse's attention is suddenly attracted he is unfortunately completely oblivious to all else, and a plastic bag that someone has carelessly discarded can cause him to shy right into the path of oncoming traffic. The horse has almost all-round vision, an important asset for a grazing animal, but he doesn't appear to be able to focus well on distant objects. The horse that appears to be looking into the distance, ears pricked, is actually mainly listening. Our aim is to reassure and desensitize him and to try to make him trust our judgement rather than his own.

Things that may unnerve him:
• bright colours, but also white objects
• shiny things, e.g. plastic bags
• black rubbish bags
• wet logs
• long waterproof coats, big hats
• parked vehicles
• dogs
• umbrellas

When Riding Keep calm and don't 'shy' yourself. If you tense up and 'hang on to the front end' you will only convince the horse that he is right to be concerned. Talking to him calmly and patting him may be all that is needed to reassure him. Check that you are sitting straight and central in the saddle, both legs stretched down with a deep heel (especially the side away from the fearsome object) to help you keep your balance if he jumps sideways. Keep your legs close to the horse, ready to react. Try not to tip forward or to turn your upper body out and pull his head towards the object (easier said than done). Keep your inner shoulder back and ride positively forward. Avoid fixing your inner hand to try to hold the horse – it can make him feel trapped and make things worse. Never punish a horse for shying. It simply reinforces his fear and makes him associate the situation with pain. The occasional impudent horse who is playing games with his rider can be corrected with firm quiet riding and maybe a stern voice, if necessary.

Left
When riding on public roads it is important to be seen. This horse and rider are wearing an array of fluorescent gear, all of which is available from saddlers.

Opposite
Out for a hack: there is nothing nicer than taking your horse out for a ride. It is enjoyable for him and is an excellent way of getting him fit. If possible, always ride with a companion in case of accident.

Chapter Fifteen
OUT AND ABOUT – COMPETING

To find suitable shows, look through horse magazines and local newspapers. Posters advertising shows are often displayed in saddlers and livery yards. If you belong to a riding club or group you will be informed when shows are to be held in the form of regular bulletins.

If you require transport, arrange it well in advance. If hiring, check that the vehicle is suitable beforehand. Send off for schedules and check what qualifications are required to enter a class. Make sure you dispatch your entry forms in good time and remember that more time is needed to process the various classes if it is a big show. Some you can enter on the day: this is a fine if you have doubts concerning the weather or state of the ground; however, you may have a long wait, particularly in the case of show-jumping.

Check that your tack is in good repair and bring a spare pair of reins. Ensure that you have the correct equipment and clothing for your particular class. Bring plenty of water and buckets. Also bring cooler or anti-sweat rugs and rugs appropriate to the weather and a set of warm and waterproof clothes for youself.

It is important to carry good first aid kits for both yourself and your horse, along with all relevant vaccination certificates, membership cards, rule books or dressage test sheets. Bring a complete grooming kit, including hoof oil and spare plaiting equipment to give him a final groom. (Top competitors even bring a spare set of shoes!) In addition, don't forget a haynet and feed for your horse for when he has finished work.

It is a good idea to bring a friend to help out and cheer you on, especially if you are jumping.

On the day Horses are quick to associate changes of routine with going out for the day and some will get very excited and agitated. Keep to his usual routine as far as possible and give fresh water and feed at least one hour before travelling, checking that he is absolutely healthy and sound before leaving the yard. Allow extra time for plaiting or to fit equipment on an unusually fidgety animal. You may well be all fingers and thumbs being slightly nervous yourself.

Travelling and arriving Choose the smoothest route, avoiding roads that twist and turn as well as places where there may be traffic hold-ups, and allow ample time. In case of breakdown, avoid unloading your horse onto any kind of road and never do so on a major one, unless the traffic has been stopped both ways. It follows that you should carry a mobile phone, if possible.

When you arrive, park somewhere in the shade if at all possible and out of the wind if it is cold. Avoid parking too near the exit. Check that your horse is in good condition after his journey and give him some water. Lower the ramp of the horsebox to allow ventilation but don't open the gates until you intend to unload him. For safety, only open the top doors of a trailer.

Once unloaded, walk the horse around to loosen him up. It is fine to tie him to the container but never leave him unattended. Never tie a horse to an unhitched trailer as he is quite capable of pulling it over on top of himself. Don't tie him up within kicking or biting distance of other horses, or leave the rope too long – he may get caught up in it and panic. Don't allow him to graze: he could pick up an infectious disease; give him a haynet if he is not going to be working for a while.

While someone is minding your horse, locate the secretary to obtain your number and pay your fee if entering on the day. Find out what ring you will be riding in and whether or not the class is running to time. Walk the course.

You can feed your horse between classes, but allow two hours to elapse before each class; offer water frequently but withhold for one hour before fast work. Letting him pick at a haynet will keep him settled, but avoid letting him eat more than a couple of pounds (a kilo or so) in the last hour before start to work-in and no hay for four hours prior to fast work.

Above
This horse and rider are clean and tidy and ready to take part in their showing class.

Left
Just arrived: these two are still in their travelling gear. Never tie a horse to an unhitched trailer. It is quite possible for a horse to pull it over on top of himself. Don't leave unattended horses tied up at shows.

Travelling Equipment

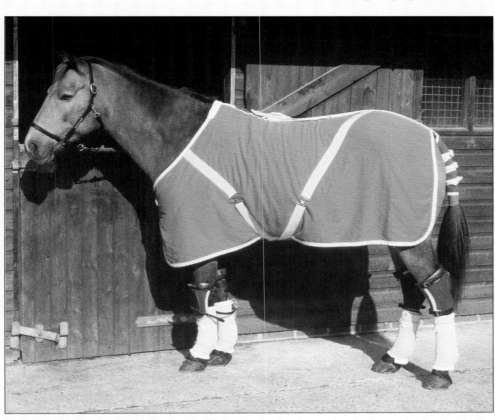

Left
It is most important that the horse has adequate protection while travelling as he could easily damage himself. However, equipment must be correctly fitted as boots and bandages that slip or overtighten can cause more damage than no protection at all. Extra protection such as over-reach boots and a poll guard are also a good idea.

Above
A tail bandage with a tail guard over the top protects the horse's dock and tail hair.

Below
A horse needs time to become accustomed to new equipment. Hock-boots will protect the joints from friction or a blow but can at first upset a sensitive horse, causing him to kick out.

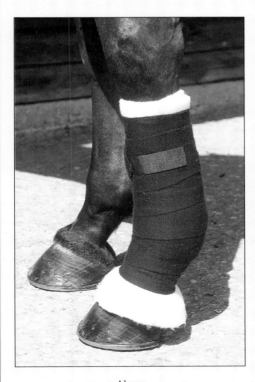

Above
Travelling bandages protect the lower leg and coronary band. All-in-one travel boots are a popular alternative but must be well-fitting or they may slip.

Above
In the event of a horse falling during loading or travelling, it is likely that the knees would be badly injured. It is therefore essential that they are adequately protected with well-designed knee-boots.

Dressage

Don't enter more that three classes and make sure you know the times of your tests in advance. Working-in is most important and should include plenty of loosening and suppling work. You will learn the amount of time you need from experience – 20–45 minutes is usual, depending on the horse. If in a large field, don't just wander about: practise the correct-size shapes, concentrating on the way of going rather than over-practising the movements. Practise specific ones once or twice to reassure yourself; if you know your horse slows down too much in the arena, try working him at a slightly faster pace and vice versa. It is a good idea to work-in as near to the arena as you are allowed to familiarize and settle the horse. Remember to use only the tack allowed for the competition. If you are unfamiliar with riding in a grass arena with boards, try to practise first at home: you could improvise with poles on the ground to mark out the arena. Watch that you don't look down and get drawn too deep into the corners.

Check the surface in the arena: if it is deep or heavy, take care not to overdo the working-in or you may lack sparkle in the test.

Make sure that you know your test: you can have someone read for you but only as a prompt. Tell the steward that you have arrived and keep an eye on the person in front of you.

It often happens that a horse and rider, going perfectly well together, can fall apart on entering the arena. A young horse, especially, needs to enjoy being in the ring. Both of you can get stage-fright – help your horse by trying to be relaxed, reassuring him as much as possible and gaining confidence from the fact that you have already practised the tests at home, working out how to prepare for and make the most of each movement. Don't get paranoid about the areas you both find difficult – focus on the positive. If you mess up one movement, forget it, and concentrate on the next. It is very easy to freeze and merely steer through the movements instead of riding as you normally would to maximize your performance. Smile, especially at the judge, and look up. With experience you will find your own recipe for

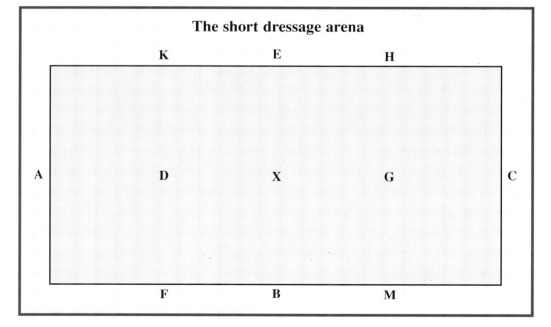

The short dressage arena

K   E   H

A   D   X   G   C

F   B   M

success. Focusing, concentrating, breathing, relaxation techniques and visualization are all skills which may help and can be learned.

After the test, learn from your marking sheet and compare it with your previous efforts, remembering that working with others can lift your performance and teach you a lot.

Dressage to music This is great fun: choose one or more pieces for each pace. There should be clear transitions (not a fade-out) between pieces where the pace changes. Try to change pace at the end of a phrase and plan a proper finale. Keep the volume steady and keep to the same key throughout if possible. Classical music is generally preferred but modern music that matches the horse's paces and programme may go down well. Vocals usually get a mixed reception: they can be either very successful or totally misfire. If the timing is for four and a half to five minutes, aim at four and three quarters, as different surfaces ride faster/slower.

Plan your programme to complement your horse, remembering to include all the compulsory movements. If you are unsure of your ability to perform one movement (such as lengthened strides) sucessfully it may be worth including two attempts to increase your chances of giving a reasonable performance. Successfully ridden movements in a difficult order or pattern will gain more marks as long as you do not exceed the requirements.

Use the music to show off your best paces such as a crescendo for lengthening, or a quiet interval for the walk. The movements should express the variations in the music.

The movements should flow and be balanced in all directions. They do not necessarily have to be identical and you do not have to use the markers. Make two to three tapes as a back-up in emergencies, indicating the points where you enter or when you salute, etc.

Practise thoroughly and learn every nuance of the music so that you are ready to improvise if the movements and music do not quite match up on the day: check the new copyright rules with the show organizer.

Opposite
Competing at dressage at the local show is fun as well as good practice.

Right
The finished product!
Nicole Uphoff and Rembrandt.

Long-Distance Riding

This can be tremendous fun and is a way of setting a goal without many of the pressures of other competitions.

At top level it consists of fixed speed rides and various types of race rides, taking as long as 24 hrs or more. In the former, prizes are awarded for completing the course at the required average speed with maximum veterinary marks. The horses are checked at intervals throughout the course for their fitness to continue and are assessed at the finish for soundness, for speed of recovery to normal temperature, pulse and respiration and for injuries, including any swellings or rubs from tack. Race rides work on a 'first past the post' or 'fastest time' system, but the many veterinary checks ensure the horse's well-being and the fitter the horse the sooner it will be allowed to continue at each veterinary 'gate'.

At lower levels, sponsored pleasure rides of 8–32 km (5–20 miles) – with or without optional jumps – and official training rides of 32–48 km (20–30 miles) at 8–10 km/h (5–6 mph) are ideal for newcomers to the sport. Horses should be 6 years old or more for rides of over 32 km (20 miles). Endurance horses do not usually reach their peak until 9 years plus and too much work at a young age can cause strain that may shorten their working life.

Endurance horses are usually quite small and often have Arab blood. Strong feet and straight action are important to cope with the different types of going and terrain without sustaining lameness or brushing injuries. A sensible temperament, willingness to go forward and good basic schooling are other important factors.

You do not need any special facilities, just access to bridleways and quiet roads. If you live in a very flat area it is worth travelling to the nearest hills to accustom your horse to steep inclines; but be careful not to undertake too much hill work suddenly.

One of the advantages of long-distance riding just for fun is that you do not need a special or expensive mount. Half the pleasure of owning a horse is developing a relationship with him and enjoying the hours of preparation as well as the actual rides. Almost any shape and size of horse can be used as long as it is fit and sound. Get to know your horse's most comfortable pace. Many will swing along in a ground-covering trot while others are happier alternating walk and canter. Learn to feel when he is tiring and never put on pressure uphill.

Before your first ride, if you normally hack alone or with one or two others, see how your horse reacts when hacked out with a larger group. Big gatherings are always exciting but not everyone will be considerate, especially on an unofficial ride. Most horses enjoy working in company but some can be overwhelmed and behave badly as a result. The sight of horses up ahead in the distance or others galloping past may well incite your horse to charge off in hot pursuit. Sensible companions are a great help but

they need to have a similar length of stride to avoid the freer-moving horses being constantly held back. Pick the best going on the flat or gentle uphill inclines for fast work; take your time on hard, stony or rutted going and heavy, holding clay.

Warming up properly is just as important as with any other discipline. With steady animals this can simply mean walking round for ten minutes and then taking the first couple of miles very steadily. If you are aiming for a faster average speed or you know perfectly well that initially your horse will want to get going and be difficult to settle, then do a thorough warm-up to avoid injuries to muscles and tendons. Bear in mind that galloping off at the start will not endear you to your companions and you may well end up with a lame horse.

Above
Long-distance riding is becoming a very popular sport. The best types of horses for this are Arabs, which have incredible speed, stamina and strength. This is champion long-distance rider Debi Gordon and her Polish Arab, Redman

Opposite
Taking part in a rodeo is one of America's favourite equestrian pastimes. The rider must have incredible balance and stamina to stay in the saddle.

Show-Jumping

As a rule, two classes on one day are ample. Be alert so that you know when to put your numbers down at the collecting ring. Make sure you always walk the course: you have a very limited time in which to do this and it is not good enough to take a quick look from the ringside. Make sure you know the rules for the different types of classes.

Working-in Be confident and alert by being aware of your horse and his requirements. Allow a minimum of 20 minutes to warm up. If it is cold and you have to wait, make sure that you keep your horse warm; put a rug over his quarters and keep walking round, then trot and canter, and possibly jump a fence, just before entering the arena. If there are flags by the practice jumps, only jump with the red to the right.

There is no need to jump a lot when working-in – some horses are better jumping a number of small fences to loosen up, though this will excite others. Always start small and then either gradually build up or take just one or two bigger fences, perhaps an upright and parallel, if available. Watch that you don't circle across in front or behind a fence when other people are jumping.

Walking the course This is a vital aspect of show-jumping and should be treated as seriously as the actual jumping. Concentrate, walking the entire track as you will ride it, and run through it in your head. Check to see if you can use a marker of some sort behind the fence to help you straighten to it. Note where you might need extra power, for example, at a big parallel or where extra control is required, such as at a tight turn. Avoid getting fixated on the 'bogey' fence and check the strides in related distances and combinations. You should decide in advance the number of strides you should ask for. Look out for and make a note of anything that may alarm your horse and any fences with coloured fillers that may unsettle him so that you are prepared to cope in advance.

Don't forget to walk insignificant fences – they are usually the ones you will knock down. Also note at start and finish where you must pass through the markers or electronic beams.

Check the jump-off course, at the same time looking for tighter turns where possible or where to go wide for the sake of a young or inexperienced horse.

Watch a few people negotiate the course to see how it rides and what the going is like.

Get to know good venues – ones with large rings or an indoor arena with a good surface for winter shows. It is important to have a sufficient working-in area. Look for well-built, inviting courses with efficiently managed class numbers which keep to time. Small arenas of poorly built courses encourage stops and run-outs and discourage fluent riding.

Wait for the bell but be ready: you only have a limited time to start before elimination. The horse might hang back to the collecting ring;

don't anticipate trouble in a negative sense but be forewarned and ready to ride extra positively without getting paranoid and making the horse wonder what is so difficult about the next obstacle.

Young horses Simple flowing courses are required with not too many bright fillers to start with and very tiny ones, if possible. Solid, well-built fences which are infilled are much more inviting than jumps consisting of only a few poles while a variety of fences will provide the young horse with the full gamut of experience.

Before you compete, practise with small fillers at home and lots of different colours placed at the sides then gradually to the middle of the fence. If you have no jumps at home, it is possible to travel to venues and hire them, or local shows may let you school for a fee after classes have finished if they are not dismantling the fences straightaway. If you have any problems, it is a good idea to get the support and advice of an instructor to give confidence to both you and your horse.

Opposite
U.S. Olympic rider Leslie Lenehan riding Charisma.

Below
Polo is not a sport for everyone and it is very expensive. The rider requires several ponies for a season which are specially bred for the job. They require exceptional stamina and fitness.

Cross-Country

Hunter trials These are courses of natural obstacles of a type you might meet out hunting.

One-day-eventing This consists of a dressage test and a round of show-jumping followed by a course of cross-country fences. Official one-day events offer consistent quality of venue and course building.

Smaller events and hunter trials vary considerably in their standards but the majority are well and safely run; nevertheless, check the going carefully for holes or uneven ground either side of fences. Also note that flimsy fences are more dangerous than strong solid ones as horses have little respect for them and tend to take liberties.

Look out for protruding nails and that jumps are not sited near dangerous fencing such as barbed wire. Make sure that the surrounding area has been made safe and that any hazards such as cattle grids have been fenced off and that gates leading onto open public roads have been closed.

Walking the course Look at each fence from a distance to judge what the horse's first impression will be. Look for line and guiding markers, checking that landmarks are not movable. Look for anything dangerous, as mentioned above. In wet weather, bear in mind that the going will get worse as the day goes on and decide in plenty of

time whether it is safe to continue.

Decide on the appropriate speed of approach for different types of fences. Note what follows after the jump: remember that the horse does not know if the fence has a drop landing or a tight turn following it.

After you have walked the course, picture the track you have chosen in your mind and ride the approaches and landings in your head. Make sure you check out any alternatives on the day. The ground conditions, as well as the way the horse is feeling, could well dictate a change of plan.

Make sure that all your clothing for each discipline is prepared well in advance and that you know your dressage test and have walked the show-jumping course.

Below

Horse and rider in balance at the gallop: Mary King and King Kong at Windsor, England. The three-day event is gruelling for both horse and rider and requires perfect fitness. The horse must be talented in all three disciplines, show-jumping, dressage and cross-country.

Opposite

A lady's hack showing class. A row of immaculate hindquarters enhanced by pulled tails and 'chequer' and 'sharks' teeth' markings. The shapes are drawn using a comb or brush against the lie of the hair or you can use a patterned stencil for a similar effect.

Showing

If you are new to showing, visit a selection of small riding-club shows and watch the various classes to see what is involved and whether your horse is suitable for a particular category. If you are doing well at local level and would like to try the larger shows, go to some, and learn from the way that professionals produce and ride their horses, then have a go yourself. (Get someone to video you at a local show so that you can see where improvements can be made.)

The basic criteria for a show horse, whether in-hand or under saddle are good conformation and clean limbs, free of lumps and bumps, be they natural blemishes or due to wear and tear. He will require a good free action, straight movement and a sound temperament and attitude to the job.

In addition, the horse needs to be the right type for the particular class. Some lovely horses seem to just miss falling into a category and fashions subtly change over the years. Generally speaking (rightly or wrongly), a good 'big 'un' will beat a good 'little 'un'.

What is required of you and your horse will vary depending on the type of class, but there are certain basics that will always apply.

A show horse should have beautiful manners, stand rock-solid still to be mounted without being held, and move out of line at a touch. He should be active, forward-going and enthusiastic, but should never pull. He needs to carry himself

proudly and move in balance with very little help from his rider and accept different riding styles with equanimity.

The level of schooling needed will vary depending on the class. A hunter, for example, needs to be a straightforward, comfortable, obedient ride, with an excellent gallop. The hack, or riding horse, should be exceptionally well-balanced, supple and responsive and show great finesse and elegance.

The horse should move freely and walk and trot up in a straight line. Try not to drag his head round to the side and make sure you are fit enough to keep up! The judge won't be impressed by a horse that is being dragged along looking like a drunken sailor. Equally, an over-fresh animal might look very impressive as he prances by but if he refuses to trot evenly or stand still to be inspected he is unlikely to be well placed.

He must stand still and alert, ears pricked (a handful of grass or a sweet wrapper helps!). Usually, horses are stood up with the legs nearest the judge a little spread, which gives a better picture.

As you can imagine, such polish doesn't develop overnight. Long hours of schooling and practice go into producing the apparently effortless performance of both the in-hand and ridden show horse.

Of course a show horse needs to be well

schooled but he must also get used to riders of all shapes, sizes and abilities as well as both sexes. (A horse always handled and ridden by a woman may well be nervous of a male judge.)

He needs to be full of life and have that indefinable 'presence' that will make him stand out in a crowd but still be calm when an air balloon passes overhead or the hound parade commences in the adjoining ring. Rearing, or napping, generally means instant expulsion from the ring and bucking is much frowned upon. There is much skill in keeping a highly-strung horse controlled but still retaining its *joie de vivre*. Too much schooling and too many shows can produce a jaded or neurotic animal who may also lose condition mid-season. A good part of the showman's skill is juggling the feed and exercise to produce a fit, well-muscled animal which carries plenty of condition and top line without being too fat.

Turn-out is very important. The rider must be tidy and clean with well-cut, well-fitting clothes. Anything overstated, such as large buttonholes or floppy hair ribbons, are out. The horse should be spotless and shining, his tack neat, well-fitting and suitable for the class. No self-respecting hunter would be seen in the delicate bridlework and velvet browband suitable for a hack or riding pony. If you are small, make sure your saddle and stirrups are big enough for a larger rider.

Ringcraft is a subtle skill which you can learn from watching top competitors. Here are some guidelines:
• Place yourself between horses that are of lesser quality and ones that are of a different colour so that your horse stands out in contrast.
• Avoid getting stuck behind a sluggish or naughty animal.
• Give yourself plenty of room but never overtake in front of the judge; some people think it will get them noticed – it will – for all the wrong reasons. Instead, cut the corners or go deep into them, circling or overtaking when the judge is looking elsewhere.

Keep an eye on the judge and steward for instructions but don't make it obvious. Make sure both you and your horse stay alert in the line-up and don't stand too close to other horses. Your individual show should be short but polished. Evaluate how best to use the available space and make sure you show all the paces and canter on both reins. Remember that no one knows your intentions, so improvise if the horse does something untoward. If a gallop is expected it is usually executed along the back of the ring. Accelerate smoothly, leaning forward just a little, and show a few really big free strides before gradually easing back to a balanced canter. However hard you may be working, smile, and make it all look effortless!

Preparing for a Show

Trimming

Most horses look tidier carefully trimmed, although certain breeds such as Arabs and native ponies should always be left as nature intended.

A pulled, thinned mane is neat and easier to plait. Back-comb the hair and pull out a few hairs at a time. If the horse objects there are special tools available which make the job less painful.

When pulling a tail, take the hairs mostly from the sides down to create a smooth, neat shape.

Use scissors and comb to remove any excess hair from jaw and heels.

Right
This pony is neatly plaited and wearing a double bridle ready for his showing class.

Opposite
A well-groomed competitor preparing to enter a riding pony class.

Plaiting the mane

1 Make sure that the mane is thoroughly clean and combed through. Divide the mane into bunches and secure with rubber plaiting bands. Small, tight plaits will enhance a thick short neck. Looser and larger plaits will make a long thin neck look more attractive.

2 Starting at the top of the neck, plait each bunch right down to the end making sure that it is neat and tidy.

3 Using a needle and strong plaiting thread, secure the end. Remember to choose a thread to match your horse's mane colour.

4 Turn the edges of the plait under to secure and neaten the end.

5 Roll or fold the plait under until it forms a neat bobble. Make sure that it is tight before securing it with the needle and thread.

6 Finally, carefully trim off any excess thread.

Plaiting the tail

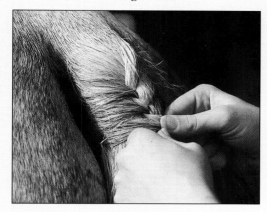

1 After thoroughly brushing the tail, begin to incorporate small sections of hair, starting at the top of the dock. Take small even sections into the centre, plaiting it in. Carry on to the end of the dock.

3 Take the long section plait and tuck it under. Secure with a needle and thread, or if you are in a hurry, a rubber band as pictured below. With practice you will be able to keep the sections of hair neat and tight all the way down.

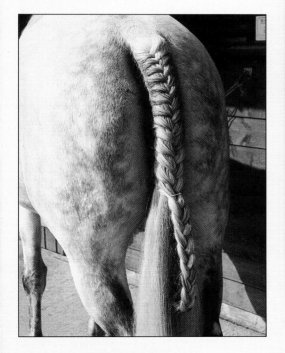

2 You will be left with a long bunch of hair: carry on plaiting this right to the end. Secure with a rubber band or plaiting needle and thread.

Clothing

When competing at shows, however small, the rider is required to wear the correct clothes. This usually consists of beige jodphurs or breeches, long leather boots, a white shirt and tie, or stock, a hacking or show jacket, gloves, and a hard hat. As you progress in the particular area of your choice you will find that more and more specialist and protective clothing is required. For example, when riding cross-country and in show-jumping you should wear a more secure skull cap as well as a body protector. When showing, make sure that you have the correct clothing for the particular class you are entering.

Abscess A localized accumulation of pus.

Action The way in which a horse moves its legs at each gait, e.g. freely and straight.

Aged Any horse older than eight years is said to be aged.

Antibiotic A drug that kills bacteria.

Bacteria Microscopic single-celled organisms that live in or on larger creatures such as the horse.

Bars (1) The hard stretches of gum between the last incisor tooth and the first molar tooth on which the bit rests. (2) The ends of the hoof wall, which extend from the heels towards the centre of the sole.

Bascule The rounded shape a horse makes when correctly negotiating a jump.

Bone The substance that makes up the skeleton of the horse. The word is also used to refer to the circumference of the leg just below the knee, as an indication of the horse's potential weight-bearing capacity.

Boxy feet Narrow, upright feet with small frogs and closed heels. Feet of this shape can cause problems because they do not absorb concussion efficiently, putting excessive strain on the legs.

Breaking out When the horse begins to sweat again after exercise when it has already cooled down.

Breed A variety of horse (or other animal) consisting of a group of individuals that share the same genetic and physical characteristics and pass these to their offspring.

Bringing up from grass Bringing a horse to live in a stable when he has previously been living in a field at rest. **Letting down** is the process of reducing a horse's level of fitness to acclimatize him to living out prior to a period of rest.

Brushing Wounds on the inside of the fetlock joint caused by the edge of a shoe or rough clenches on the opposite foot. Can also be caused by bad conformation and faulty action.

Bulk The greater proportion of the horse's diet that has the highest fibre content, such as hay and grass.

Cast (in a stable or box) When a horse lies down or rolls in a confined space and is unable to stand up again because he has rolled too close to the wall or his feet have become stuck (under a manger, for example).

Cast, to When a shoe comes off accidently rather than having been deliberately removed.

Cereals Grasses that have been developed to provide seeds for food, e.g. oats, barley.

Chaff Chopped oat straw or hay added to short feed to aid digestion.

Circuit-breaker A device fitted in a wall-socket. When electric clippers, for example, are plugged into it, the power is cut off if there is an electrical fault, preventing an electric shock.

Clench During shoeing, the part of the nail which is left projecting from the wall of the hoof is twisted off and then bent over to secure the shoe to the foot.

Cold-blood A heavy horse descended from the primitive forest horse of northern Europe.

Cold hosing The use of a constant stream of cold water to reduce inflammation.

Collected (paces) The horse's steps are shorter, active and springy. More weight is carried by the hind-legs and the forehand becomes lighter with the neck raised and arched.

Concentrates Foods providing high levels of nutrition in a small volume, e.g. oats, mixes, cubes.

Concussion (1) The shock of impact as the horse's foot hits hard ground. (2) Result of a blow to the head.

Condition The horse's level of fitness or fatness. 'Hard' means the horse has well-toned muscles and no surplus fat. 'Soft' means unfit with very flabby muscles and carrying surplus fat.

Conformation The horse's general shape and make-up.

Croup-high When the horse's hindquarters are higher than the withers.

Dam A horse's mother.

Deep litter A way of bedding down horses by removing droppings only, before adding clean bedding on top.

Dishing A fault in a horse's action in which he throws one or both legs out to the side instead of in a straight line.

Double bridle A bridle employing both a snaffle (bridoon) and a curb bit, with two sets of reins.

'Ewe neck' The muscle at the top of the neck is underdeveloped and the muscle underneath is overdeveloped, giving an upside-down appearance.

Extended (paces) The maximum length of stride. The horse stays on the bit, in rhythm, lengthening its frame without falling onto the forehand.

Falling in Compensation through stiffness or lack of balance when a horse turning on a circle or round a corner moves his shoulder in and comes off the true circle.

Fibre Also known as cellulose, this is the tough material that strengthens the leaves and stems of plants. Grass and hay are examples of high fibre feeds or roughage.

Folic Acid A vitamin needed for blood cell formation.

Forage Bulk food such as hay.

Fungal spores The microscopic particles by which fungae spread through the air and which can cause allergic reations in horses.

Gait Walk, trot, canter and gallop are the basic patterns of leg movements common to all horses.

Galls Swellings or sores caused by rubbing from poorly fitting saddlery.

Gamgee Cotton wool strengthened with gauze.

Going The condition of the ground and how it affects a horse's movements.

Hacking Riding a horse in the countryside for pleasure.

Half-bred A horse which has one Thoroughbred parent and one of a different breed.

Hand A unit equal to 10 cm (4 inches) by which horses are measured.

Haylage A way of preserving grass which is similar to hay, but higher in protein. It is virtually free of dust and spores and is a good alternative to hay for horses with respiratory problems.

Heating A way of describing feed with a high energy content which can give rise to excitable behaviour.

Hollow The horse's head is high above the vertical and resisting the bit, causing the back to hollow. An incorrect way of going.

Hot-blood A horse of Thoroughbred or Arab breeding.

'Hot up', to A horse who becomes unduly excited, when ridden is said to 'hot up'.

In-hand A way of leading a horse from the ground (particularly in showing classes).

Interval training Scientific method of developing fitness while minimizing strain on the horse's limbs from excess galloping. A programme suitable for a one-day-event (training level) would consist of walk breaks of 3 minutes, canters at 400 m/minute (15 mph). Take pulse and respiration after each canter and 10 minutes after finish.

Start with 2 x 2-minute canters. Build up to 3 x 5 minutes, including 1 minute at half-speed gallop in the final canter. Proceed as follows: Day one – work day; day two – 1 hour walk/rest at grass; days three and four – varied hacking, schooling, jumping.

Lactic acid Produced in the muscles during exercise but can cause pain and damage to the muscles if not quickly removed by the circulation.

Light of bone A term used to describe limbs that are too slender, lacking sufficient strength for the horse's build.

Loosening work Large easy shapes ridden in working paces with the horse in a relatively long, low outline. Used to warm the horse up for more demanding work.

Manège An enclosure where horses are schooled.

Medium (paces) Longer steps which maintain rhythm and still feel 'uphill'.

Nappy Used to describe a stubborn, wilful horse, who will not go in the required direction.

Near side A horse's left side.

Off side The horse's right side.

Over-face, to To ask a horse to jump an obstacle which is beyond his capability or level of training.

Over-reach (to) When the horse strikes the front heel with the hind-foot causing injury.

Over-tracking The horse's hind feet step in front of the prints of the fore feet.

Pace (1) The speed of a horse at a certain gait. (2) A specific two-beat gait where both legs on the same side move at the same time.

Parasite A living organism that lives on and off another creature, providing no benefit to its host.

Pony A fully grown horse not exceeding 14 hands 2 inches (1.47m).

Poor doer A horse who requires a large amount of feed to stay in good health or maintain condition.

Pulling (mane or tail) Removing excess hairs from the underside of the mane and sides of the tail to improve appearance.

Pus The matter formed by accumulation of bacteria and dead white blood cells when there is a localized infection.

Quartering A quick grooming to tidy up the horse, usually before exercise.

Self-Carriage When the ridden horse carries itself in a well-balanced manner, light in the forehand, without relying or leaning on the rider's hands.

Serpentine A ridden movement consisting of a series of same-sized semi-circles that are performed in opposite directions down the length of the manège.

Short feed Feed such as oats, barley and maize which is given in small quantities.

Sire A horse's father.

Sound A horse that is healthy in wind, eyes, heart and action.

Stale, to To urinate.

Stallion An uncastrated male horse.

Staring (coat) When the hairs of a horse's coat are dull and standing up instead of lying smooth and looking glossy.

Strapping A thorough grooming after exercise when the pores are open.

Strike-off Transition from a slower pace into canter.

Tack Equipment or saddlery worn by a horse.

Tracking (up) The horse's hind feet step into the prints of the fore feet.

Turn out, to To put a horse out in a field (out to grass).

Type A group of horses which are of broadly similar body shape and size but which are genetically dissimilar.

Under- or over-horsed Riding a horse which is not suitable for your level. (1) Under-horsed: too old, quiet or small. (2) Over-horsed: too young, lively, strong or large.

Vaccination Immunization or inoculation against specific diseases such as tetanus or equine influenza.

Vice An undesirable habit.

Warm-blood A horse whose ancestors include both cold-bloods and hot-bloods.

Wisping or strapping A way of massaging the horse's muscles and improving circulation using a pad made from leather or twisted, plaited hay.

Working (paces) The everyday pace for warming up, exercising and working young horses. The horse's frame is quite long and the steps active and free.

Some U.K./U.S differences in terminology

U.K.	U.S.A.
Brushing	Interfering
Anti-sweat rug	Sweat sheet
Bad doer	Unthrifty horse
Bandage	Leg-wrap
Maize	Corn
Cubes	Nuts or pellets
Dishing	Paddling
Equiboot	Easyboot
Fetlock	Ankle or joint
Gamgee	Cotton encased in gauze
Going	Footing
Good doer	Easy keeper
Headcollar	Halter
Horsebox	Van
Lead-rope	Lead-shank
Numnah	Saddle pad
Over-reach boot	Bell boot
Plait	Braid
Rasping	Floating
Rug	Blanket
Shelter	Run-in shed
Stable	Stall
Stables/stable yard	Barn
Stall	Horse box
Surcingle	Over-girth
Veterinary surgeon	Veterinarian